From Joining the RSO Network to Putting Wrapped Candy on a Guest's Pillow, *START YOUR OWN BED & BREAKFAST BUSINESS* tells you how to do it right!

- Young mothers can build exciting new careers—right in their own homes!

- New homeowners can help pay mortgages, taxes, and other expenses.

- Retired persons can put empty bedrooms to use—and make fascinating new friends.

- Even full-time workers can supplement their incomes.

"Beverly is doing for Bed & Breakfast in the United States what AAA has done for motels."
—Ruth Wilson, Director
Bed & Breakfast Texas Style

". . . The perfect tool for the B&B home."
—Pat Hardy, co-author of
So You Want to Be an Innkeeper

"Beverly Mathews is *the* authority on the gentle art of Bed & Breakfast hosting. Her enthusiasm and commitment to this lovely European concept is contagious. I am delighted that so many others will now benefit from her expertise and creativity—and join our ranks!"
—Trudi Alexy, President
California Houseguests International, Inc.

Start Your Own Bed & Breakfast Business—Earn Extra Cash from Your Extra Room!

~ Beverly Mathews ~

Photos by Austin Walker

PUBLISHED BY POCKET BOOKS NEW YORK

Another *Original* publication of POCKET BOOKS

 POCKET BOOKS, a division of Simon & Schuster, Inc.
1230 Avenue of the Americas, New York, N.Y. 10020

ISBN: 0-671-60037-0

This is a revised edition of the book originally published in 1984 by Rocky Point Press.

First Pocket Books printing October, 1985

10 9 8 7 6 5 4 3 2 1

Acknowledgments

This book is dedicated to the thousands of Bed & Breakfast hosts and travelers (now and in the future) who are helping to make our world a warmer place, and to:

- My many students, for questioning.

- All of the hard-working B&B reservation services for their important role in the amazing growth of B&B in America.

- Simone and Pierre, the perfect reasons for B&B.

- Florence, for her professional wisdom.

- Austin Walker, for his photos that captured the feeling of B&B.

- My children—Bill, Tim, Karen, and Lauren—for understanding and tolerating all of my crazy projects.

- Stacy Puls, the busy editor who took time to listen, liked what she heard, and made it all happen.

- And to Wally, my husband, who believed in the book, encouraged me, and found Stacy.

Foreword

When I started the Tourist House Association of America in 1975 and published the first Bed & Breakfast directory, B&B in this country was just getting started. At last there was an alternative to hotel high-rises and motel monotony. You can imagine my pleasure as I've watched the B&B movement sweep the country. When my *Bed & Breakfast, U.S.A.* directory first appeared, it listed 46 homes in 20 states; the newest edition gives the traveler access to over 12,000 B&B homes in 50 states, and has a readership of 100,000!

If you have tried B&Bs as a guest (or are interested in making a little extra money) and want to start your own B&B, you will find that *Start Your Own Bed & Breakfast Business* answers all your questions. Beverly takes you by the hand, giving you step-by-step instruction, clearly pointing out all the pros and cons of each decision you make. Her advice is accurate and practical. If I were to begin again in the B&B business, this is the book I'd buy.

Welcome to the wonderful world of B&B hosting, and good luck!

—Betty R. Rundback, Director
Tourist House Association
of America

Contents

Introduction

Bed & Breakfast, or B&B as it is known in Europe, has achieved a respected place among travel-housing options, particularly in Great Britain. There, discreet little signs mark the private homes that offer inexpensive and unpretentious bedrooms—with breakfast the next morning—for the traveler. Hosts are accustomed to receiving guests without advance reservations. The low cost makes this a popular way to travel, and minor inconveniences (such as sharing a hall bathroom) are soon forgotten when weighed against the warmth and hospitality extended by B&B hosts.

Bed & Breakfast has suddenly become popular in the United States as well. In this country, however, one cannot simply pop in off the street at will. Reservations must be made in advance, usually by mail. And with typical Yankee ingenuity, Americans have embellished the B&B experience to such a degree that the traveler does not necessarily save money by choosing this type of accommodation. Some commercial inns in the U.S. have as few as two bedrooms and prices as high as $250 per night. Many require weekend reservations up to eight months in advance! While this is not the norm, it shows that innovations in innkeeping have taken American B&B out of the realm of the "boardinghouse" and into that of new chic.

B&B in America can be either an inn experience or a stay within a private home, with host and family in residence. This American "Homestay," a balance between the original European version of B&B and the costlier commercial inn, is the nearest thing to our British B&B cousin. One common denominator among B&B inns and B&B Homestays is breakfast. Each offers a morning meal at no additional charge. Other amenities vary, but the attempt to provide personal attention and genuine concern to the individual traveler is paramount.

11

Start Your Own Bed & Breakfast Business is primarily concerned with the Homestay. Because of considerable overlap in service and intent of both types of B&B, however, this book is of value to potential innkeepers as well. (Note the many periodicals, organizations, and seminars mentioned throughout, and the special chapter designed primarily for innkeeping hopefuls.)

Hosting in private homes in this country is done in an almost clandestine manner due to severe zoning restrictions as well as a concern for personal security. Signs are limited to commercial inns. Most hosts rely on reservation service organizations (RSOs) to publicize their homes and to protect their anonymity.

Would-be hosts approach the prospect of entertaining strangers with a mixture of excitement and fear, particularly when faced with the added problem of language and cultural differences. I hope to give the reader contemplating such a venture some insight into situations that might be encountered. Some of you will have individual and specific questions I will be happy to answer. See the forms provided at the back of the book.

New reservation (referral) services open daily, and though I include a list of such organizations in a later chapter, it is bound to be incomplete and outdated even as I write. Should you wish the most current information on B&B reservation service organizations handling your particular area, please send the application form (again, at the end of the book). I will return a list of any changes that apply to you.

My family has been hosting B&B guests for five years, and I have been giving my startup seminars and workshops to potential hosts for four years. We find the interest in Bed & Breakfast growing at an astounding pace. Countless books have been written extolling the virtues of commercial inns. Travel sections of bookstores have innumerable guides to guesthouses (Homestays). A network of Bed & Breakfast Homestays stretches across the continent. Homestays are available in almost every town—and certainly in every city—in America. Associations are springing up in almost every county to help the traveler and host find one another.

Networking has been a prime reason for the proliferation of B&B in our country. In my classes I stress the importance of sharing. I ask you, as I ask my students, to keep in touch. Keep me updated on the growth of B&B in your area. Let me know how you are doing, what progress you are making, what roadblocks you have managed to hurdle (and how), and when you open for business, send brochures. Brag a little; brag to me a lot! Put me on

your mailing list and I will pass along the news to fellow travelers. They in turn will spread the word. B&B may be in its infancy here in America, but what an energetic and exciting period of growth has begun. Join the Bed & Breakfast boom and share in the fun!
Good luck.

Beverly

Start Your Own Bed & Breakfast Business—Earn Extra Cash from Your Extra Room!

CHAPTER 1

What Is a B&B?

Man has been in a constant state of movement ever since Adam and Eve left the garden of Eden. With the exception of the rare hermit, people consider communication and linking an integral part of life. In the past, the need for information was fulfilled by the itinerant traveler, who provided news for the settler. The settler, in turn, offered rest and repast. During the development of our colonies and the push west, for example, beds were offered to weary strangers who provided a link with the world left behind; food and information were shared—and cherished. Students of social history are fascinated to learn that Spanish padres of the early eighteenth century deliberately spaced California missions a reasonable day's journey apart, so early western travelers could both rest and share their news.

As industrialization progressed, short-term accommodations were needed in communities that sprang up along the routes of the stage, the riverboat, and the railroad. As factory workers arrived in the growing cities, guest homes and boardinghouses emerged as a form of inexpensive housing. Boardinghouse guests later proved an important source of income for homeowners during the Depression. Farmers opened their doors to city dwellers during sultry summers in order to supplement an often meager income, creating an inexpensive vacation alternative and a wonderful experience for the sidewalk-bred child. My own husband's father met his future wife while vacationing as a paying guest at her family's Connecticut farm.

Immigrants to the United States have brought with them memories of B&B in England, Scotland, and Ireland, *pousadas* and *estalagems* in Portugal, *paradors* in Spain; *pensions* in France and Italy; the *gasthaus* of Germany; and the *minshukus* and *shukubos* of Japan. And today, with the emergence of low-cost travel for the middle class, Americans are discovering the world themselves, often staying in foreign B&Bs. Is it any wonder that Bed & Breakfast would eventually become a viable alternative to the American hotel or motel option?

Travelers in America have a choice between staying in a B&B inn or in what is generally referred to as a Homestay. The latter is a private home located (usually) in a residential neighborhood, where the owner rents extra bedrooms and provides breakfast to paying guests. The guest becomes almost a member of the family, since common areas are shared with one another.

B&B inns are commercial operations, generally offering more rooms and services, with the owner living in separate quarters (or even off the premises). Often, a manager will take care of the day-to-day operation of the inn, and many times ownership will be shared by a group of people (usually in larger operations). B&B inns must meet stringent local and state regulations. Guests have specific common areas for their use. Though a warmth and personal interest in the guests exists (unlike a motel or hotel), there is naturally less intermingling with the host-owner than is found in a Homestay, where the guest is directly a part of the family's life. The inn must operate in a more businesslike way, adhering to stricter routines, inasmuch as a staff is generally involved. The homeowner can afford to be more flexible, since less is at stake financially. The homeowner, though, usually realizes less profit, his or her "business" is generally a sideline or hobby.

Host Benefits

Whether their operations are set up as B&B inns or B&B Homestays, hosts receive benefits far beyond the dollar income. First-time home buyers find B&B hosting an excellent way to help pay the enormous mortgages and taxes with which they are suddenly confronted. Homebound mothers who are B&B hosts can become part of the "outside world" without leaving the house. Singles can supplement their incomes and still go off to work while a B&B guest is visiting. Retired persons with large "empty nests" can use those empty bedrooms and make new friends from around the world; long-term friendships are often created. Children involved with the B&B experience receive a special benefit—they are often exposed to the culture and language of other countries, learning more than they could in school, or from a textbook or TV show. They will realize how much alike people are, whatever their origins, whatever their governmental philosophies. B&B cannot play the game of United Nations, but it can make a very real difference on a one-to-one level. It enriches our view of the world.

Guest Benefits

The B&B traveler receives advantages, as well. Parents feel more secure knowing their children are traveling B&B and staying in a home environment. Children and baby-sitters, in turn, feel free to call the B&B owner with detailed messages for vacationing parents. When guests move on, they are confident that the B&B owner will be able to forward information (and may have even been an active participant in making the next reservation).

Women traveling alone find more than safety a reason for the B&B choice. The convenience of a laundry room, an ironing board, hair rollers—all of those bulky items one needs but won't pack—to say nothing of usually warm and individualized decorating that mass-purchased hotel furniture can never duplicate—are just a few of the reasons more and more women, and more business travelers of both sexes, are traveling B&B. Traveling businesspersons who must do most of their work early in the morning by telephone (due to three-hour time differences from coast to coast) also find the B&B a happy change from their former hotel/ motel environment; the added integration with a family helps take the curse off the constant feeling of being "on the road." Homestays are truly homes away from home. I know of traveling salespersons who actually leave a suitcase at their regular B&B stops! One visitor celebrated a family birthday with us and became an instant relative.

Proximity to hospitals and nursing homes is an excellent reason for choosing B&B for people visiting patients or desiring to save money during a pre-op testing period. Wedding guests can be provided with necessities and even amenities in a B&B, without getting in the way of the wedding party. The father of the bride can save quite a bit of money by putting up guests in B&Bs instead of hotels. And wedding parties themselves are often held at B&Bs. Many people are at a B&B while attending to unhappy business—funerals, ongoing illnesses, relocating aging parents, continuing therapy, relocating their *own* families. It helps immensely to have a friendly face, a pot of tea late at night, a possible confidant. This is hardly available from room service at a comparably-priced hotel.

Older people, youngsters away from home for the first time, foreign travelers in a new land, the handicapped in need of a few special considerations—these and countless just plain "curious" travelers are learning that B&B can be the solution to many a potential problem. It is like having your own personal concierge.

Equally important, every B&B experience is different, while most hotels and motels are predictable. If a traveler needs that sense of constancy, then B&B is not the right choice for him or her. But if he or she is looking for an added dimension to a trip, a change from the old routine, then B&B is definitely the answer—for one can return time and again to the identical B&B and find even more changes. As I said in the introduction, B&B is an evolving business. We are learning each day from other operators and from the traveler. We actively seek out what the guest wants and do our utmost to grant guest wishes. Fairy godmothers we aren't, but we pride ourselves on coming close.

The Importance of Reservation Services

Most B&B hosts and guests in the United States are "matched up" by Reservation Service Organizations (RSOs). Most hosts find RSOs an indispensable part of running a B&B Homestay.

My introduction to hosting was through a very selective membership reservation service. Since both host and guest alike would be carefully scrutinized before joining, there was a strong sense of security for me, a novice at this "business" of throwing open my doors to perfect strangers.

Since that day in 1979, the B&B movement has accelerated at an incredible pace, and literally hundreds of RSOs have been formed. I believe it almost essential to work through a reservation service unless yours is a commercially zoned home (and legally allowed to hang out a sign and advertise aggressively). I think it would be next to impossible to make money without one.

What Is an RSO?

An RSO locates, screens and matches guest with host. In some cases, it collects both deposit and payment, takes out a commission for its service, then passes the balance along to the host prior to guest arrival. Elimination of these financial details makes hosting quite pleasant, more like that of hostess to friends from out of town. In some cases, city bed taxes are collected by the RSO as well. Any additional chargeable services are strictly between host and guest. The RSO receives no commission other than for securing accommodations.

Some reservation services charge a one-time fee to cover the cost of inspecting homes and creating directories of member-home descriptions. These booklets are distributed widely to the media and are sold to individuals curious about the kinds of homes and locations that are available.

All RSOs take a commission, which can range from 20 percent to 35 percent. I feel this fee is well deserved; it covers mailings, phone bills, advertising and promotion (the lifeblood of the RSO), insurance, membership in countless business and professional associations, dealing as an intermediary in all the little details of arranging compatible bookings, and often includes a payment of 10 percent to travel agents, as well. This last expense is an important one that more and more RSOs are recognizing. Travel agents are an important source of room rental, but they have traditionally given business to hotels. Unless B&Bs are willing to compete with a commensurate commission, there is no reason for the travel industry to change an old habit. (Travel agencies are an obvious target for publicizing "in concert" the wonders of B&B: groups of hosts, RSOs, or associations might contact major agencies throughout the country, advertise and publicize in travel industry magazines and newsletters, and generally spread the word that commissions can, in fact, be earned when booking clients into the world of B&B.)

Working with an RSO

Different RSOs handle reservations in different ways (see Chapter 7, "Reservations and Checkout"). Do some research, and you'll be able to find several RSOs that can provide you with guests in a manner you're comfortable with.

Many students ask if I pay commission to an agency when guests they've matched me with return. Quite honestly, I have very few returnees. That is not to suggest that my home is undesirable (I know of just one unhappy guest in over five years). We simply seem to receive travelers who are on a once-in-a-lifetime trip. Were they to try to re-book direct, however, I would definitely feel a moral obligation to deal with the agency that had made the original connection, or forward an unsolicited commission.

Some reservation services specialize in one small part of their home state. Others are trying to be global in scope. Still others are developing computer software to enable them to match traveler and home in the same way that passengers book plane tickets. However they do it, I commend all for making the B&B boom what it is. Without the RSO, we would still be scrambling for the occasional guest, and never have the visibility now afforded.

I wish there was enough business so that I could work exclusively with just one RSO. It would make bookkeeping far easier. At least at this point, however, each RSO has its own special contacts and never have I had to decline a guest due to conflicting reservation requests. So, for the time being, I will continue to work with helpful people from several RSOs and hope we will all thrive.

I am a bit concerned, though, that too many RSOs may develop, and create a glut, with the result that none will prosper, some will fall by the wayside, and those remaining will have to struggle to stay afloat. Most B&B experts agree that the more than 300 now in existence are sufficient unless, of course, more specialty RSOs emerge. See the accompanying section on RSOs for a listing of RSOs currently operating in your state. Check also those that work nationally and internationally. And don't forget to look at the list of specialty agencies. You may qualify for membership in all three categories. Because of the constant state of change within this business, no lists remain accurate for long. See the end of the book for a *Reservation Service Update* form.

Working Independently

Independent hosts must do their own advertising, promotion, and screening of guests, collect both deposit and balance due, handle the myriad of reservation (and cancellation) details, and be available to answer phone calls day and night, unless equipped with an answering machine with a separate phone line for this purpose. Most unnerving to me, however, is that the host must now reveal an address to the world at large. I, for one, want to keep a low profile—and feel that the services provided by the RSOs justify every cent I pay in commissions.

For those of you who want to work independently, I wish you great success. It certainly can be done. Be prepared to spend a lot of time on the telephone and at the typewriter. You will have to persevere to get publicity, and spend money on advertising. You will have to join every organization available, become more active (and thus more visible) in your community, and publicize yourself in all of the guidebooks that include your area, promoting all the time. But it *can* be done. I know of hosts who stay adequately busy working on their own. I also know of those who work both on their own and with RSO help. How busy you are as an independent will depend on the time and energy (to say nothing of the expense) you wish to exert.

Independent hosts may keep their privacy intact by taking reservations through the mail only, using a post office box as a mailing address. The home address is given only at the time of confirmation of deposit. This will help alleviate the problem of unexpected arrivals. It will also keep the number of unwanted phone calls to a minimum. Private mailbox service is available in most communities today. However, the U.S. Postal Service still offers the best bargain. I pay twenty-two dollars per year for a small mailbox. Large parcels are delivered to me by means of a slip placed in the box reminding me to claim these larger items at another window. A plus to having a post office box is that mail will be forwarded for up to six months at no extra charge. If you are even thinking about using a U.S. post office box, pick up a request form right away. The wait can be a long one at the busier stations. You will be notified when one becomes available, and can make a decision then.

CHAPTER 2

Getting Started

Dealing with the public in any capacity can be a constant test of one's virtues. Dealing with the public in your own home creates additional burdens that could disrupt family harmony; what was begun as an adventure in togetherness might create a permanent marital rift. After all, the castle is being invaded, and privacy is being threatened. Before considering any home-based business, you should make a careful study of the personalities of the people to be involved and your housing situation.

The Perfect Host:

☐ Has the ability to get along with others.

☐ Enjoys working at home; socializing with co-workers is not too important.

☐ Has a spouse and children who support the idea of having a B&B . . . strangers in the home . . . sharing the castle.

☐ Basically likes and trusts people.

☐ Is curious about the world and recognizes that other cultures have their own, quite different ways.

☐ Is adaptive . . . can adjust quickly to change.

☐ Can handle simple bookkeeping.

25

☐ Has extreme patience (or can *appear* unruffled) when dealing with the public.

☐ Is willing, when necessary, to do menial chores in the name of "business" without feeling a loss of dignity or self-esteem.

☐ Is interested in the B&B experience as much as in the income it may or may not generate.

☐ Will be able to juggle work hours to allow sufficient family time.

☐ Can organize time.

☐ Is enthusiastic and energetic about the business.

☐ Is a good housekeeper, if not a great decorator.

☐ Is aware of and can adapt to special guest concerns/needs such as allergies, dietary restrictions, handicaps.

☐ Can boil an egg and make a good cup of coffee.

☐ Is an instinctive judge of people.

☐ Though flexible, can stand up for convictions under pressure.

☐ Can't wait for the first guest to arrive, and anticipates the next with enthusiasm (no matter what happens!).

☐ Has a sense of humor!

A Host Should Look For a Guest Who:

☐ Is looking for new experiences in travel-housing.

☐ Has a sense of adventure.

☐ Has a sense of humor.

☐ Arrives with no preconceived notions . . . wants to be surprised.

☐ Has notified host in advance of arrival of any allergies, special needs, and services required.

☐ Brings the host no unexpected (or unsuspected) baggage—such as unwanted children, unallowed pets, smoke (of any kind), allergies or other afflictions unless well stated in advance.

☐ Is not looking for maid service and special attention, but wants to become a (distant) member of the family.

☐ Prefers charm and hospitality to room service and bellhops.

☐ Can tolerate sudden minor emergencies, not unlike what happens in his/her own home.

☐ Will speak up when things are not as they should be or were pictured to be.

☐ Is essentially independent in thought and action.

☐ Is basically informal or can adapt to an informal living situation.

☐ Is thoughtful. Will call host in advance of arrival to specify anticipated arrival time; will call again should plans change or delays develop.

☐ Will have own transportation or the ability to use public means.

☐ Likes meeting new and different people.

☐ Can handle less privacy than accustomed to in hotel/motel living.

☐ Will judge each B&B experience on its own merits, and try again if the first was not a great experience (the media sometimes glamorizes B&B to a goal almost unreachable by the average homeowner).

☐ Is willing to drive a few miles out of the way to look for a new experience. (Some vacationers actually remember their B&B stays better than the guidebook highlights.)

Just as there is no such thing as a perfect guest, neither is there a perfect host. The best one can do is try to anticipate potential problems and bypass them before the fact, attempt to retain a sense of home for both the guest and the family members, and create ways to guarantee privacy for everyone concerned. Keep a sense of humor and learn to compromise. If, for example, a smoker is inadvertently booked into your non-smoking B&B, tell him or her that smokers are *welcome* in your home, but ask that smoking be confined to the patio and other outdoor areas.

Assess Your Home

When contemplating starting a B&B, discuss potential problems with the family, and make everyone part of decision and policy making, as well. Considerations:

☐ Is there a secluded portion of the house where your family can have total separation from guests? Spouse and children should not be obligated to entertain guests or *behave* as guests in their own home.

☐ Is there an area of the house where family children can be comfortable with their friends without explanation (or possible embarrassment) of strangers in the home?

☐ Is there a family or television room available solely for family use? Nobody should be forced to change TV or music habits, as long as the noise level doesn't interfere with the peace of others.

☐ Are any items needed by the family in potential B&B rooms?

☐ If so, can they be located in another place? (Out-of-season clothing, dead-storage items, a desk in use—these are a few examples of personal things that might be needed and inaccessible during rental periods.) Guests might feel uncomfortable surrounded by intimate family objects.

☐ Can family bathroom necessities be conveniently shelved away from the room(s) used by guests? One gets an odd sensation when opening another's filled medicine cabinet.

☐ Does the house have a separate entrance for guest use? Though certainly not essential, if one can be set up, both guest and family will find the convenience/privacy a great advantage. It will also be a selling feature to travelers concerned with too much "togetherness."

Assess Your Location

Transportation, or the lack of it, plays a disproportionate role in the success or failure of any trip. It can also make a difference in the role a host will play, as well as how much income can be generated from a B&B.

Though our home is located within walking distance of city transportation, I must confess we encourage our guests to have an automobile at their disposal, even if that entails renting one at the airport. The majority of our visitors arrive by car, probably due in part to the reputation (not totally deserved) of Los Angeles' public transit system. The bus system is actually quite a good one and gets you anywhere you wish to go—eventually! Unfortunately, as in most sprawling cities, the wait can be interminable, taking up precious time that could be put to far more productive use sightseeing. I feel great compassion for the guest hoping to "see" Los Angeles in a two or three day stay. We've been here for nine years and are still learning!

I vividly remember English guests who were left in limbo for several hours—some thirty miles away—simply because they'd

lingered over Sunday brunch and missed the last bus home. Public transportation seems to slow down drastically once the weekday work rush ends, leaving evenings and weekends a problem for the car-less guest. Since cab fares can be devastating to a travel budget, the remaining option is to walk home after dark in a dimly lit, poorly marked, and totally unfamiliar neighborhood some distance from the nearest bus stop. Urge your guests to have a car!

Hosts may arrange to meet travelers at the airport, but I strongly advise checking your auto insurance policy first. My personal choice is to keep a supply of taxi phone numbers and bus schedules available along with local tour brochures.

When assessing your location, things to consider include:

☐ Can driveway guest parking be arranged so that family autos are able to move in and out freely without being blocked? This may sound petty, but envision an irate husband, late for work and unable to get out of the driveway without awakening an exhausted paying guest. Serious! Or,

☐ Can ample off-street parking be provided for guests, even if this means parking your own car on the street? Neighbors know your automobile, but might complain about strange license plates, particularly if business is thriving. Most localities have been versed by the neighborhood watch groups sponsored by the police departments to watch for irregularities. One obvious and noteworthy item would be an out-of-town license. Numerous strange cars could create quite a commotion along with zoning problems.

☐ Is your home accessible to major highways or throughways? Even though a bit off the beaten track, if directions are simple to follow, strangers are more likely to make reservations with you.

☐ Are there businesses and associations nearby that might be able to use reasonably inexpensive rooms for their own purposes? See Chapter 8, Publicity and Promotion.

☐ Are you centrally located? This can be an asset or a negative. An asset, when convenient to everything . . . a negative if street noises disturb sleeping guests or if your guests really want to "get away from it all."

☐ If parking facilities don't exist, can you arrange something with a nearby church or other organization at nominal cost to guests?

☐ Is public transportation within reasonable walking distance?

☐ Is any major business or tourist attraction nearby?

☐ Will guests have access to restaurants without driving interminable distances?

☐ Are neighbors compatible? Nervous? Jealous? Paranoid?

These and other considerations will crop up when discussing your neighborhood with the other members of your family. Don't arbitrarily decide B&B is not for you should possible problem areas surface. If you pinpoint a problem, try to resolve it. Turn the negatives into positives. If, in fact, your house is out in the "boonies" as one of my students stated, I told her to stress the advantages of living near the city but with the peace of the country; breathe the clean air after fighting the smog-filled freeway; ride at the neighborhood stable while less fortunates are fighting the freeway system. In other words, there is a reason why *you* live there; pass on the secret (and its advantages) to the weary traveler.

Gauging the Family Attitude

It is inevitable that one or more members of the family will be concerned about the prospects of hosting. The newness of the B&B movement is in itself a reason to wonder about B&B. Reactions of peers to the decision will bring on varied questions suggesting anything from poverty to avarice. Doomsayers will welcome the chance to relate the latest escapades of the local rapist and present dire warnings of rising crime statistics. Needless to say, if you have any fear of strangers (recommended though they may be), paranoia about your possessions, or a strong fear of being robbed, choose another sideline business. Nothing is worth the sleepless nights.

Encourage family members to participate in hosting, but don't force the issue. Negative attitudes will eventually surface, and probably at the worst possible time.

Specify to what use the B&B income will be put. Let every family member have a voice in the decision (every family member, that is, who *agrees* to happily participate).The anticipation of a vacation will do wonders to turn a snarling teenager into a gracious host.

Above all, if there is any indication that guests are putting a strain on the family, curtail all hosting as soon as possible unless the source of irritation can be located and corrected. Unhappy family members can do more harm than good in the long run. The mood is pervasive.

Questions the family might ponder include:

☐ If we have to give up use of a bathroom, who is responsible for moving things in and out?

☐ Who cleans the guest dishes? Bath? Laundry?

☐ Do the children share in the proceeds of B&Bing?

☐ If not now, when? To what degree?

☐ Are the teenagers able to realize that slight inconveniences will be felt by all family members, but the income is needed to sustain or increase expendable income—used for, again, *all* the family?

☐ Young children in the family may fear strangers. How does one handle the constant coming and going?

☐ There may be times when family relatives will want to visit while paying guests are in the house or anticipated. Will feelings be hurt?

☐ Grown children may occasionally find "their" bedrooms occupied by strangers when arriving home for a sudden, unannounced visit. How does the family cope?

☐ Occasional family emergencies will come up. Will other members help with the hosting at such times?

☐ Guests may not object to family pets, but will the pets object to *them?*

These and dozens of other thoughts may come up. I don't mean to suggest that each and every problem should be met and resolved head-on. Just be aware that much give-and-take is a part of this new family sideline business.

If you think you—and your family—are ready to embark upon the B&B hosting adventure, the next eight chapters will help you get ready to open your door to your very first guest!

CHAPTER 3

Important Business Concerns

I wish there were some way to bypass this particular section. Rules and regulations become the main stumbling block for many an aspiring entrepreneur, but, unfortunately, they are also the most important areas to be conversant with. The following is intended as food for thought, but *you must get professional advice from a trusted accountant, attorney, insurance person and/or local officials.*

Since B&B is relatively new in this country, zoning and tax laws are not quite ready for us. Neither is the insurance industry. In fact, when you contact almost any level of government regarding B&B questions, the answer will often be ". . . what?" One can only hope that by the time this book is in print someone in authority will know that a B&B is not a boardinghouse, that transients off the street are not encouraged, that reservations are an integral part of the B&B operation, that B&B is being pursued as a business and not just a hobby, and that no, B&B is not a sublet situation. Most owners are hosts-in-residence who are trying to engage in a home-based business, thus needing protection against liability.

☐ ZONING . . . Each community has its own zoning ordinances. As a general rule, a local planning board sets goals and develops a growth plan. The zoning board develops and enforces regulations created to achieve these goals, and the appeals board exists to waive the regulations. Contact the local zoning board or city hall to learn what applies to your area, and what measures can be taken to appeal, get a waiver, or obtain a variance, should such action be needed. Most zoning officers will not chase after people who aren't bothering anyone, so be aware of (and eliminate) any nuisances that might provoke your neighbors. Most important, try not to create problems when they have not been addressed! Keep a low profile, for obvious reasons.

☐ Have adequate off-street parking for yourself and your guests.

☐ Try not to generate excessive traffic or noise.

☐ Maintain specific hours for parties and/or playing of music.

☐ Schedule swimming and other backyard activities for reasonable hours and insist on normal noise levels.

☐ Have pool men and gardeners arrive during normal business hours. If they refuse, get another serviceperson.

☐ Consider getting a post office box in order to avoid overloading your mailman.

☐ Keep your yard (particularly the area facing the street) in perfect condition.

☐ Set out trash cans at the appropriate time and remove as soon as emptied.

☐ If guests bring pets, make certain they are confined to an enclosed rear yard, and that the guest is responsible for maintaining a quiet animal.

☐ Do *not* hang signs advertising your B&B unless allowed in your zoning. Even so, keep signs discreet and in good taste.

It is obvious that all of the above suggestions are simply what would be expected of a good neighbor under any circumstances.

☐ **HOUSE INSURANCE** . . . Read your homeowner's policy carefully. My particular policy automatically includes coverage for two paying guests. Some RSOs provide (for a fee) insurance for their member homes, but generally only for those guests booked directly through their company. Make sure you know exactly what (and whom) is covered by your RSO and your insurance company. Ask your insurance agent about the cost of an "umbrella policy" and/or additional rider for business use for occasional paying guests.

☐ **AUTOMOBILE INSURANCE** . . . Rarely will an auto insurance policy cover liability arising out of the ownership or operation of a vehicle while it is being used to carry persons or property for a fee. If you are considering transporting guests to the airport, on guided tours, or for any purpose for a fee, make certain you are covered in case of an accident. The "umbrella" policy might be able to be set up for this purpose. Discuss a special rider with your agent. Indicate that this use of your car will be minimal, if at all, in chauffeuring your paying guests. Any extra income ideas utilizing the car could become major problems in the event of even a minor accident. If considering renting or lending your personal automobile to guests, discuss this with your insurance broker as well.

☐ **BUSINESS TAX AND PERMIT** . . . Every community has different regulations regarding this matter. The city clerk can provide information or direct you to the proper source for facts regarding possible transient occupancy tax, a license to do business, under what circumstances they might be necessary, and costs (generally quite nominal). Know the facts before starting.

☐ **FEDERAL INCOME TAX** . . . You may be liable for paying income tax as a B&B owner. On the other hand, there may be excellent tax credits (refer to Chapter 4, Money Matters).

☐ **RELEASES** . . . On page 36 you'll find a sample of the release we ask our guests to sign. It is not a legal document (see an attorney before drawing one up). It just might make someone think twice before considering litigation, though.

Naturally, a good insurance policy, with a clause providing for paying guests, is the preferred safety valve. We have both insurance coverage and a mandatory release form.

☐ **NAMING YOUR B&B** . . . As in the case of any business, unless the surname of all owners is listed in the company name, a *fictitious business license* (DBA) must be obtained. A name that suggests the existence of additional owners (such words as "Company," "& Company," "& Sons," "& Associates," "Brothers") must be filed (in most states) with the county clerk of the county in which the registrant has his principal place of business.

Generally, the fee (in an amount of approximately ten dollars) must be filed within forty days from the time business commences. Within thirty days after the statement is filed, it must be published in a newspaper of general circulation in the county in which the principal place of business is located. An affidavit of publication shall be filed with the county clerk within thirty days after the completion of publication.

Release

During the period of our stay in their home at 1111 Madrid Avenue, Los Angeles, California, we will in no way hold Mr. and Mrs. Walter Mathews or any member of their family liable for any illness, accident, injury or loss that may occur to us, and shall use their premises at our own risk. We agree to be liable for all damages we cause to their property beyond reasonable and normal wear and tear.

_____

NAME(S)

_____

ADDRESS

_____

CITY

_____

STATE (COUNTRY)

_____

Many newspapers will take care of this *complete* transaction for you. Prices vary, so shop your local papers. They will request a nominal fee to have the county clerk search to see if the chosen name is available for your use (i.e., not already being used by another business). If it is available, you must then place four classified advertisements at intervals, giving the name(s) of the principal(s) involved. The cost for these ads can start at thirty dollars for the package, so check carefully. The name is aesthetically important; choose carefully and consult Chapter 8, "Publicity and Promotion" when considering.

☐ **FEDERAL IDENTIFICATION NUMBER** . . . You need a federal employee identification number if you have one or more employees (*non*-family members—check this carefully with your accountant).

36

Most states have similar requirements. Contact your state's department of benefit payments for specific information.

In all legal matters, I strongly urge you to contact the appropriate local, county, state, and federal departments. They can be found through your local telephone directory or through the nearest office of the Small Business Administration, as well as the local chamber of commerce. Libraries are an excellent source of information. Librarians consider it a challenge to research problems. Get to know yours personally.

For Safety's Sake

A tired guest in a strange house late at night is the perfect candidate for an accident. A prime concern of hosts is to maintain the B&B in the safest possible manner, without becoming paranoid about everything (insurance companies tend to pay better attention to careful homeowners and may bend a bit in your favor if you can show a list of obstacles—or potential ones—that you have avoided). In addition to insurance company rulings, for your own safety, consider the following:

☐ Keep walkways and steps clean and dry.

☐ Trim low-hanging branches wherever people might walk.

☐ Have front porch and hallways well lit at night.

☐ Provide night lights in bedrooms and baths. Keep on twenty-four hours when guests are present.

☐ Install smoke alarms in kitchen and bedroom halls even if not mandated.

☐ Keep fire extinguishers in kitchen and each bedroom closet. Maintain equipment as indicated on manufacturer's label.

☐ Area rugs should have non-slip backing.

☐ Tub and shower should have floormats. Both rubber and disposable paper mats are available.

☐ Post pool (and hot-tub) rules in a conspicuous place.

☐ Keep life jacket or long pole at poolside.

☐ Provide children's water safety jackets if you allow youngsters in your B&B.

☐ Police, fire, ambulance, and paramedic phone numbers should be on or next to every telephone, along with "911" information if "911" is available in your area. Additional copies of this information should be prominently displayed in each guest room (inside the closet door?)

☐ Confine smoking to one outdoor or common room area, if allowed at all. "No smoking" applies in many commercial inns, but prevent problems by clearly stating your sentiments on brochures and reservation forms.

☐ Bedroom windows should be easy to open in case of need for escape or rescue.

☐ Single or double dead-bolt locks are recommended for exterior doors.

☐ Sliding glass doors should have metal screw pins or key-controlled window-locking devices.

☐ Decals should be placed on sliding glass doors to prevent quickly moving people from running into them. Placed at several levels, children as well as adults will be warned.

☐ Guests should be able to lock bedroom doors from within.

CHAPTER 4

Money Matters

As with any business, setting up a B&B means making decisions on financial matters and being aware of other important considerations: setting rates, figuring out ways to improve business, coming up with ideas for making extra money, becoming conversant with tax laws, and learning where to turn for help.

Setting Rates

No Homestay host can possibly rely on B&B as the sole source of income. It is absolutely a sideline business, a way to provide additional income from ingredients already available—you, your home, and your spare bedrooms. (See Chapter 9, "B&B Host Profiles," to see the incomes others derive from B&B hosting.) The number of rooms available for rental purposes, the amount you charge for these rooms, and the business activity you obtain will naturally affect the total annual receipts. Room charges will be contingent on many things:

Available Space

B&B can be found throughout the country in every conceivable (and inconceivable) location. Large homes with numerous empty rooms are the obvious preference since you can then provide more choices for your guests. Two bedrooms will accommodate a large family or unrelated parties traveling together, as well, of course, as two independent couples. The option of king or twin beds offers a sometimes critical alternative. I cannot count the number of reservations I lost before equipping our second room with twin beds.

However, B&B can be found on houseboats, as well as in one-bedroom Manhattan apartments. Many of us will sacrifice privacy for adventure and location. So don't arbitrarily decide that yours is an unsuitable candidate for B&B.

My most vivid travel memories, some bad but mostly good, were not of the cities visited, but of the accommodations we had along the way. I cannot recall the names of many hotels, but I can recite details about the unique B&Bs encountered. How could one possibly forget Sunnyside, a one-time potato chip factory in Sunnyvale, California? The kitchen was originally the factory garage. A hole in the middle of the room used to be a grease pit. The hole remains, but now serves as a pantry—shelves line the pit, and the cook descends by ladder to the brick floor below to get supplies. I entered what I believed to be a bedroom closet only to find myself in a freight elevator, once again lined with shelves. A library ladder provides access to one of the largest personal libraries I've ever seen. And the hosts will even give you a ride on the still-working elevator (to nowhere, I sense), should you ask. I also remember everything we had for breakfast, the baked brie appetizer served one evening to lift our spirits, and the gem of an inn sitter. We never met the owners of Sunnyside; they were out of town. But I feel as though we are longtime friends. Evidence of their unusual lifestyle was all around us. Needless to say, few of us live in potato chip factories, but if we did, I wonder how many of us would have had the creativity and imagination to envision what could be done, and at relatively little cost. Again, *don't dismiss your home as a possibility for B&B. Almost anything can work well, and often does!*

Location

Location will play a major role in your B&B's earning potential. The number of visitors will vary widely from town to town and state to state. Are you located near major corporations, universities, hospitals, retirement homes, or other sources of potential repeat business? A home within walking distance of a large hospital or university will certainly be busier than one located in an isolated area. A B&B close to year-round tourist attractions or midway between two major cities would probably get more visitors than a seasonal resort off the beaten track.

Just as location will play an important part in the amount of activity your home may expect, it will also be a decisive factor in determining rates charged. The law of supply and demand is constantly being proven in B&B.

During the 1984 Olympic games, in anticipation of enormous crowds, reservation agencies sprang up throughout the Los Angeles area, signing on homes available for rent as well as potential B&Bs. Word spread that rooms would be at a premium—and prices being quoted were thus outrageously high. In the end, both hotel and B&B space went begging—for many reasons, not the least of which was the fear among potential visitors that they could not afford the well-publicized food and lodging costs. Many new agencies were forced to close long before the events got under way. Some agencies that remained open had to lower prices drastically before the games began. Unfortunately, the damage had been done. Many homeowners had paid fees of fifty dollars and upward to be listed with these "reservation agencies," yet were left without guests. Some of the surviving RSOs are still struggling to overcome the huge financial losses suffered. Others have given up and closed their doors. There is simply no way to guarantee that even a world-famous event will bring travelers. And the lesson learned from the 1984 Olympics is an obvious one: had room prices been lower, it is possible that many additional guests would have visited Los Angeles.

If you are located in a "country" area not far from the beaten path, with an architecturally and aesthetically interesting home and spectacular views, you can probably charge prime dollar for a stay at your B&B. If yours is the only B&B in the area to boast a certain facility or service (swimming pool, fishing equipment, picnic lunches), you have an additional advantage. But *don't forget that most people choose a place to visit before they choose a place to stay.*

Competition

How can one best set rates? I believe that market research is essential. Your B&B is being run as a business, albeit a small one. Copy successful entrepreneurs and do your research homework.

Draw a circle on a local map with the center at your house, and a fifteen-minute (fifteen-mile?) driving radius from home. Visit each motel, hotel, or other source of rooms within that circle, getting brochures, checking on available amenities, noting conveniences and proximity to additional services, and (most important) learn room rates. Do they have mid-week specials, weekend or seasonal price changes? Your prices must be competitive and reflect all of the same variables.

I recently had a taste of competition at work. One nearby motel has a minimum room charge of sixty dollars per night for a single room. We based fees on a percentage of that amount. Later, I discovered a motel just one block down the street is charging thirty-nine dollars for a single room and only forty-three dollars for a double. Needless to say, we had to do some adjusting of prices. True, each of us has different things to offer. One motel was larger, had a year-round outdoor pool, in-house coffee shop, barber service, and gourmet dining room, but the basics were at both.

Ours is a family atmosphere. We do not offer the same degree of privacy afforded in a motel or more commercial B&B inn. Antiques, lovely to us, may appear as so much clutter to others. Our casual lifestyle includes accepting a bit of dog fur and cat hair, not to mention the occasional outrageous jungle cries of a daughter's visiting parrot. No such surprises are in store for the guest down the street! The motel pool is undoubtedly larger (but overdosed with chlorine, I suspect). We can't afford to keep our pool heated. They have a manager in constant attendance, while I'm in bed early and out of the house much of the day. True, breakfast is not included in their rates, but coffee shop or room service is available around the clock. No such service in the Mathews' kitchen! One thing we have that cannot be duplicated—anywhere in the world—is us! Our imprint is all around.

Many of us think our homes are special, however, and tend to place an unrealistic value on things that hold absolutely no interest for a stranger. By the same token, occasional newcomers to hosting consider their homes less desirable than they really are, believing wrongly that they must appeal in the same manner as a commercial B&B inn. This is an equally unreal perspective. *Look at your home objectively, if you can. Try to think as a guest might. Assess both the positives and the negatives from an arm's-length view.* Get the advice of the reservation services you contact. They have seen hundreds of homes, know the going rate for B&B throughout the area, and will be able to give a fair appraisal.

Your Expenses

In fixing rates, remember the various costs that must be covered, not the least of which is the percentage paid as commission to the RSO that finds you travelers. All operating costs should be considered before arriving at the rate needed to show a profit (or even a break-even point) per guest. *All costs should be estimated at a per room, per night basis.* Items to be considered include:

☐ Commission charged by RSO. (Should you feel that the recommended price quoted by a reservation service is too low to earn a profit, work out a way to lower costs per room, if it all possible. Otherwise, you will be working at B&B as a hobby, and a losing hobby at that. The other option would be to insist on a higher cost per room. Unfortunately, the RSO relies on reasonable room charges to create business, and if your prices are too high, they must naturally steer inquiries elsewhere. Another course to follow would be to bypass the RSO altogether, enabling you to keep the entire room fee. That, however, entails other expenses and problems dealt with in the section on RSOs.)

☐ Cost of food.

☐ Cost of fuel (gas, water, power).

☐ Depreciation of linens, dishes, TV, any items used by guests.

☐ Cost of bathroom supplies.

☐ Cost of laundry supplies, cleaning materials (for bedroom and bath).

☐ Percentage of membership fees, advertising costs, etc., allocated to B&B rental.

☐ Depreciation on house (get the opinion of your C.P.A. In some instances, early depreciation might cost you when you go to sell the house).

☐ Insurance.

☐ Taxes.

☐ Licenses.

☐ Auto expenses for business (depreciation & mileage).

☐ Maintenance and repairs.

☐ Office supplies (stationery, postage, brochures, etc.).

☐ Legal, accounting, bookkeeping expenses.

Only after all of these costs have been gauged can you truly arrive at a fair and equitable rate per room.

Varying Demand

Many B&Bs change their rates if business is seasonal in the area. Others find it best to cease operations entirely during the "off" season, using that quiet time for their own vacations, redecorating, or just enjoying a simple immediate family lifestyle for a while.

Some B&Bs offer lower rates for weekend travelers (if that is a slow time) or special mid-week prices. Use your common sense and provide discounts, if economically feasible, during the slow periods to boost business.

B&Bs that accept long-term guests may give a seventh day free, based on weekly reservations. This offer would be of special interest to large corporations housing relocating employees.

Other Considerations

The amount of money to be made hosting can never be truly determined ahead of time. Too many variables enter into the accounting. For example:

☐ Is your property in a resort area?

☐ Are hotels, motels, spas nearby that might overbook on occasion? You could do them a favor by taking the overflow.

☐ Are you willing and able to spend money advertising, promoting, garnering publicity, and joining B&B associations to become more visible?

☐ Have you contacted publishers of B&B directories to be considered for inclusion in their next edition?

☐ Have you joined community, social, and religious organizations? If so, they can help you spread the word.

☐ Are you willing to provide other services (for a fee or free of charge) to your guests that will make yours the preferred B&B within your area?

☐ Have you obtained the services of a knowledgeable accountant or attorney to guide you in the numerous tax advantages of home-based business? The many write-offs will create additional profit.

These are just a few of the questions you must ask yourself. Business is business, by whatever name it is called. The time and energy invested in assessing your home's assets and drawbacks will only return as income if spent wisely. A casual approach to B&B will create, perhaps, a hobby and a few new friends, but I am assuming that the investment made in this book is just the first of many serious steps along the way to a sideline business that may bring in financial rewards as well.

Sure Ways to Improve Business

Throughout this book I mention ways to earn more money by providing extra services for guests. However, this presumes the guests are in your home. What do you do if business is slow and the doorbell simply isn't ringing enough?

One Bed & Breakfast association offers special enticements to former guests through a regular newsletter. During the pre-Christmas weeks (when business is generally light), participating inns take guests on shopping tours, give holiday craft classes, hold cooking sessions for gifts from the kitchen, etc.—all during midweek only, for business is never a problem there on weekends at any time of the year. The same group has a bridge tournament, with guests housed at member B&Bs. This, again, is held during the week.

There is no end to special offerings that will bring travelers. Local visitors and convention bureau and chamber of commerce, as well as the newspapers, have schedules of upcoming events that might appeal to former guests: antique shows, craft events, business meetings, conventions, boat and automobile shows, etc. All are excellent sources of potential guests. Engagement announcements in the local paper indicate the possibility of visitors from out of town at the wedding. They will need a place to stay! The business section of the paper will tell of companies moving to or expanding in your vicinity. Expansion brings more employees, who in turn may need temporary quarters while looking for permanent housing. The sports page will let you know that a visiting college might require space for the athletes' families and fans. There is no end to the promotional opportunities to be found in the daily paper. These occasions are year-round and could keep yours a busy household, whatever the season.

There are numerous ways to entice guests.

Additional Money-Making Ideas

Once you've taken care of finding guests, how do you make sure they return? Recommend you to friends? Report favorably to RSOs and travel agencies? Consider offering additional services.

☐ Serve a full breakfast as part of the room cost.

☐ Allow smoking (at least in a specified area).

☐ Welcome single men traveling alone.

☐ Permit pets.

☐ Offer private baths.

☐ Keep rates low.

☐ Give discounts on long stays.

☐ Accept long stays!

☐ On a one-week booking, give the seventh night free, or allow a ten percent (or other) discount.

☐ Accept one-night stays (many hosts think this is too much work for too little reward).

☐ Arrange to pick up arriving guests, preferably free of charge, or plan to meet them where inexpensive public transportation discharges (check your automobile insurance, of course).

☐ Take guests on sightseeing tours (check insurance). Free?

☐ Deliver guests to departure site (check insurance).

☐ Read Chapter 8, Publicity and Promotion, and starting promoting.

☐ Get your imagination rolling!

While you are generating more money, guests will be getting the benefit of personalization and convenience. However, the line between offering additional services at extra cost and appearing to be greedy is a fine line indeed.

For example, if your policy is to accept young children, guard rails for a bed, cribs, high chairs, playpens, and other in-home necessities should probably be offered free of charge. On the other hand, strollers, car seats, booster chairs for use while eating in restaurants, all items not necessary to a comfortable stay *in* the B&B, would be optional "extra" conveniences that could be considered "chargeable," as would the child care and babysitting services you or your teenagers might wish to offer.

As a rule of thumb, I would charge for anything outside the usual B&B provisions that might cost you money (or wear out in time from constant use). If guest use causes depreciation and ultimate need for replacement, I would consider that a chargeable use. Remember, you are a private homeowner, not a commercial operation.

I think it is important to offer extra services if and when it pleases you. Once you find yourself feeling like a servant, B&B will lose its charm. (I know of one very successful innkeeper who is open for business only three days a week. He could be filled to capacity *every* day, but feels that three days of hosting is "fun" and anything beyond that would become "work"; he foregoes the extra income for a relaxed lifestyle.)

Suggestions for generating additional income:

☐ Pick up and deliver guests to airport, train, or bus. (Note that insurance should be carefully checked before offering any driving services for a fee. Most policies do not automatically include this option. A rider will probably be needed.)

☐ Create personalized tours specifically designed around the guest's interests. Tours might be offered at the time reservations are confirmed and could be set up with (optional) host driving or an extensively marked map and "itinerary." An innovative San Francisco cab driver has a very successful sideline business providing customized maps. Clients send him a list of interests and ages of the party, along with a check for twenty-two dollars. They receive a map of the city and surrounding areas with objectives pinpointed, along with local restaurants (again matching their taste and needs), admission fees, business hours, cab fares, availability of public transportation, and all of the other small details that can be time consuming for a stranger to find out during a short-term stay. Walking tours can be indicated, as well as places of historic (or other special) interest on the tour route. A list of local events occurring during the guest's stay are a natural accompaniment.

☐ Consider creating a sightseeing company as a sideline business. A friend of mine owns Sightseeing Surrey in Studio City, California. Her luxuriously appointed van transports groups of up to six. She has a chauffeur's license and all necessary insurance coverage. This much-needed supplement to travel choices has filled an obvious gap. If such a service is not available in your town, think about starting one. (If one is already operating, keep a supply of the service's brochures in each room. You provide guests with important information, and gain a business contact who could bring *you* business, as well.) Such sightseeing tours can be offered to reservation services and other B&B Homestays in the area. If you are successful, you might do what my friend did—join the local convention bureau and chamber of commerce, branching out in a totally new direction. A sightseeing business has the added plus of being viable even when you don't have guests; advertise through other B&Bs (for a commission?).

☐ Pick up and deliver guests to tourist attractions, business meetings, restaurants.

☐ Offer day trips to the beach, mountains, park, etc. Include a picnic lunch and accessories (beach towels, blankets, umbrellas, athletic gear).

☐ Provide laundry and dry-cleaning service. Mending.

☐ Order and pick up tickets for special events (theater, concerts, fairs). One New York reservation service sends a flyer announcing these services to all who inquire about the company. Backstage visits to meet off-Broadway actors after the performance are even arranged. The nominal charge guests incur for requesting tickets in advance is well worth the cost, since last-minute purchases (if available) will most likely mean mediocre seating at top price.

☐ Give the option of additional meals (with the family or served in guests' rooms). See section on Extra Meals (page 83) for ideas.

☐ Consider selling small toilet articles in travel/sample size—a welcome aid to haphazard packers. If these items are purchased wholesale and in quantity, you can save a considerable amount of money.

☐ Provide child care while parents tour adult areas or dine out.

☐ Allow rental of certain baby equipment not considered part of normal B&B room furnishings—stroller, car seat, baby carriage, booster chair for restaurant or automobile use.

☐ Rent sporting goods—bicycles; tennis racquets and balls; golf-clubs, balls, and cart; ski equipment; roller and ice skates; snorkel and scuba gear.

Let the Government Work for You

When a B&B is operated as a hobby, Bed and Breakfast expenses are allowable income tax deductions, but only up to the amount of income the hobby generates. Of course, all income must be reported. All profits (money earned that is over and above what you spent) are taxed, but an income tax loss may not be generated by hobby expenses.

When operated as a business, B&B will be eligible for numerous tax benefits that hobby income does not enjoy. In addition to countless legitimate home-based business write-offs you can take, you may open an IRA and, possibly, a Keogh savings account as well. Each working member of the family may open an individual IRA. Non-working spouses may also participate on a limited basis. *Speak with a knowledgeable accountant or tax attorney about these and other financial aspects of owning a business.* Don't rely on friends or writers where tax matters are concerned, particularly since tax laws are in a constant state of flux. The recent tax revisions need especially careful study. IRA, Keogh and business expense deductions are all affected. A new change to your advantage could more than offset the consultation fee.

Briefly, all money contributed to an IRA is federally *tax-deductible* the year you invest it, giving you immediate tax relief and thus reducing tax liability. The interest earned on this account is federally *tax-deferred,* only taxed upon withdrawal (which may start at age fifty-nine and a half). As in all self-employment, B&B operators may open a Keogh account, with a maximum contribution limit at this time of fifteen percent or $30,000, whichever is less. This contribution is made with before-tax dollars. The 1984 TEFRA amendment allows a twenty-five percent contribution, based on a money purchase plan. The voluntary "nondeductible" contribution of up to ten percent may be made with after-tax dollars, and is therefore non-deductible. The advantage of this deposit is that interest is tax-deferred until withdrawals are made after retirement. Again, get details from your tax adviser.

The Internal Revenue Service explains tax laws pertaining to starting a business in Publication No. 334, "Tax Guide for Small Business." It is free, and can be obtained at local Internal Revenue Service offices and at many participating public libraries. Other publications available by mail from the IRS Forms Distribution Centers include: No. 525, "Taxable and Nontaxable Income," No. 527, "Rental Property," No. 533, "Self-Employment Tax," No. 535, "Business Expenses," No. 587, "Business Use of Your Home," and No. 590, "Individual Retirement Arrangements (IRAs)". You might also want to look into:

☐ **IRS CODE SECTION 280A(G)** . . . This provides that if a dwelling unit used as a residence by the owner/taxpayer is rented for less than fifteen days of the year, then (1) income derived from the rent shall not be included in gross income, and (2) no deductions may be taken for the rental use of the residence. If rented for fifteen days or more, all income must be reported and the taxpayer is entitled to a deduction of all normal expenses.

☐ **TAX REFORM ACT OF 1976** . . . Historic landmark tax credits of up to twenty-five percent can be yours if you qualify. Rehabilitation of an approved local landmark can also qualify you for an annual depreciation deduction and other deductions based on financing and operating expenses. For information, contact the IRS and The National Trust, 1785 Massachusetts Avenue, N.W., Washington, DC 20036.

☐ **ECONOMIC RECOVERY TAX ACT** . . . Adaptive reuse (converting old, abandoned buildings into new, useful ones) may interest readers. The Economic Recovery Tax Act of 1981 gives tax credits of between fifteen and twenty-five percent for reuse of older buildings. Seek expert advice on this and any other tax questions.

☐ **INCOME TAX WRITE-OFFS** . . . Your accountant will have information in this area. For specific information, I strongly urge you get an adviser who is knowledgeable in real estate taxes. In addition, request from your nearest IRS office all literature relating to home-based businesses. In general, I deduct all costs directly connected with the upkeep and decorating of my B&B rooms, pool, and gardening (to the extent of B&B use), all books, periodicals, membership fees, commissions, publicity and advertising costs, food expenses for guests, proportionate fuel and water costs, and items such as soaps,

50

colognes, and shampoos offered for guest use. Your attorney or accountant will be able to advise on the pros and cons of deducting home office expenses and depreciating your property.

The federal government (and for that matter, the state government and city government as well) wants us all to succeed. A successful business means more tax revenue, more jobs, and additional disposable income spent in the community. This all adds up to a healthy economy. To that end, various services have been set up on all levels of government to aid the fledgling entrepreneur, as well as established firms that are independently owned and operated.

The U.S. Small Business Administration aims to help people get into business and stay there. Through management counseling and training, financial assistance, marketing and technical publications, and numerous free or low-cost workshops, start-up help is available. SBA district offices are located throughout the country and can be found in the phone book. They are staffed by experts who offer individual management assistance and consider loan applications. Attend the regularly scheduled free seminars at which professionals discuss financial and legal factors in planning your business, taxes, licenses needed, regulations, zoning, insurance, recordkeeping—all of the dull but necessary aspects of running your business.

Request an appointment with a SCORE counselor when you contact the SBA, for the Service Corps of Retired Executives is composed of hundreds of volunteers who will eagerly share their expertise in all areas of management. Counseling is available at your business location, at a local SCORE center, or at the local chamber of commerce. I know of several instances where a SCORE volunteer met clients at potential business sites. Some volunteers will come to your home or invite you to meet at theirs. This truly amazing group of men and women will give as much of themselves as they can, then steer you to others, should you need help beyond the initial counselor's knowledge.

Phone your local SBA office during the last week of each month to order the next "calendar" of nearby management training programs. Hundreds of free or low-cost classes in your area will be listed, all of which are co-sponsored by the SBA.

Write for a list of free publications offered by the SBA. Request Form SBA-115A from SBA, P.O. Box 15434, Fort Worth, TX 76119. I highly recommend you also request a copy of "Small Business Bibliography No. 2"; "Home Businesses," MA No.

1.001; "The ABCs of Borrowing"; and MA No. 6.004, "Selecting the Legal Structure for Your Firm," at the same time. Some of these booklets may be in stock at the local SBA office, as well.

Form 115B lists Management Assistance Publications that are available for a fee and can be ordered from the Superintendent of Documents, Dept. 39-CC, U.S. Government Printing Office, Washington DC 20402. U.S. Department of Commerce field offices sell these booklets, too. Check your phone directory to see if a field office is located nearby.

State and Local Aid

Most states have an office of small business or department of economic and business development. For example, in California, *A Guide to Starting a Business, Buying a Business, Financing a Business* is available at minimal cost from the Office of Small Business Development, 1030 Thirteenth Street, Suite 201, Sacramento, CA 95814. This guide lists publications available from the State Board of Equalization, which oversees areas relating to resale permits, sales taxes, and excise taxes. Collect all available literature.

Every state has a tourist office. Find out what periodicals are available regarding B&B, and request maps and special event information for your area. In addition to being useful business tools for you, guests will profit from a flow of materials about the area.

For information about locations of city or county clerks (the offices that issue new business tax and permits), the State Board of Equalization (if you plan to sell merchandise in connection with your B&B, obtain a sales tax permit from this office), or your local city hall (for information on zoning), again, check the phone book.

Progressive communities seeking the tourist dollar will have active visitor centers and/or convention centers. These are good starting points for researching community needs and procuring information about upcoming events. Local government officials will have the latest information about pending legislation and proposals that may or may not affect B&B in your town. Attend town meetings and take an active part in the community. Become visible, available, and friendly. You may need help one day.

Help from the Private Sector

Business help is everywhere for low (and often no) cost. The county bar association generally offers one-time consultation at low cost with an attorney specializing in your area of need. Young attorneys create clients this way.

Local universities and community colleges offer services at nominal cost as well. Upper-division students, in need of professional credit for resumes, are a good source of accounting, business start-up, and brochure design talent. These same schools have extension classes in every conceivable area of business. Such workshops and seminars are often given by working professionals with practical information gleaned from the surrounding community.

Small Business Institutes (SBIs) have been organized on almost five hundred university campuses to help small businesses. Senior and graduate students at schools of business administration, along with their faculty advisers, provide management counseling on-site, guided by SBA management-assistance experts. Contact the school of your choice to see if you can receive academic credit for taking such a course.

Though you may plan to keep your own books, have an accountant get you started. If you intend to use a professional book-keeper, at least learn to read the records and understand what is happening to your money. We have all heard the horror stories of widows left to decipher intricate business matters, audits of taxes prepared by a long-gone accountant, and the sudden (surprise) failure of major banking institutions. Anyone not interested in seeing how his or her money is handled is asking for problems.

No matter how simple and unsophisticated your B&B plans, keep receipts from and records of every transaction. Try to pay by charge or business check. If cash purchases are made, make certain to get a stamped receipt, noting the place and date of purchase, and itemizing expenditures. Keep these receipts separate from everyday family bills. At tax time, everything pertaining to business will be in one spot and easily totaled. You'll be surprised how tax deductible items add up over 365 days; keep even the seemingly insignificant receipts. Remember that if an audit is done, the burden of proof always rests on you, the taxpayer.

CHAPTER 5

Peace of Mind: Yours and That of Your Guests

Security

The inevitable question of home security comes up in all of my seminars; it is probably one of the first questions asked. Safety is of prime concern to everyone. It seems like only yesterday that a locked door was the exception to the rule; today, you are considered mad if you don't have two front door locks. Home security systems are successful business enterprises. Signs warning intruders have become a part of life throughout suburbia. And the abundance of dogs doesn't necessarily reflect a sudden growth in the number of animal lovers.

As I have stated elsewhere, anyone who is terribly fearful of theft or strangers should find another way to make money. Every new guest is a new opportunity to worry. Of course, a guest takes risks, too. Travelers carry valuables which they often leave in the room while sightseeing. Few B&Bs provide more than an inside bedroom door lock; guest rooms are accessible to the entire family while guests are away.

I feel that one must instinctively like and trust people to be a B&B host—or guest. Beyond faith in human nature, and the feeling that guests will respect the fact that you have opened your home to a stranger, I have no guarantees for you—nor for myself.

I can tell you that in the five years we have been inviting the world into our home, absolutely nothing has disappeared. Only one thing was broken (by a twelve-year-old; we raised the guest age to fourteen immediately thereafter), and I have received gifts from almost every encounter. I truly feel we have been the recipients of as much as we have given . . . perhaps more.

New arrivals receive a key to our home. We have a heavy brass "B" keychain (not unlike those used in European hotels) as a weighty reminder to return it at checkout time. For extra caution, there are several other options:

- Have a special guest key engraved "Do Not Duplicate." Honest locksmiths will abide by this and refuse to service potential copiers.

- Have two front-door locks and issue keys to only one. Lock both on leaving the house when guests are not in residence.

- Change the lock if you are suspicious of a guest. (Change it after he/she leaves, naturally.)

- Buy a combination lock. Consider locks with combinations that can be changed (by you) whenever new guests arrive.

- Give out no keys to the main door. Wait up until the last person gets home!

I always hope that my guests will not arrive with many valuables, and I find that today's sophisticated traveler rarely does. We offer an inside bedroom door lock (a skeleton key or door chain could work equally well), and we *could* offer the use of our bank safe deposit box. That, however, would entail the trust that *we* would be honest, and the possibility that a guest could make a false claim. Instead, we notify guests that we are not responsible for any loss or theft (just as most public establishments do).

To protect a B&B, use the same precautionary measures any other homeowner would take (see Chapter 4's insurance and safety sections). In addition, be sure that someone is at home when the guests leave, if at all possible. It is best, however, if guests have been carefully screened by you or your reservation service, for it is often impossible for working hosts to arrange their days to suit everyone's departure schedules.

Both my husband and I work, though on erratic schedules. We have said our good-byes the night before, left farewell notes, and received the same along with monies due for telephone or other extra charges (of course, you will have collected the basic room fee upon guest arrival). Absolutely nobody has forgotten to leave the key, lock the door, or clear his or her dishes. Nor has a single towel ever disappeared. Remember, B&B guests are made to feel as if they are part of the extended family, so they don't think of hosts in the same way as they would a corporate or big business entity. Who would take a friend's towel?

House Rules

Without a clear-cut explanation of your way of doing things, guests will feel uncomfortable. Each B&B home is different, and even experienced guests need to know the rules of the house. In fact, they welcome the information. And you will feel better knowing guests understand your needs and limitations.

I suggest you include important points in your brochure as well as on reservation and confirmation forms. Upon receipt of the deposit, some hosts send a "Dear Guest" letter along with the room confirmation. In this letter, include helpful facts about your home and neighborhood, as well as information about what is required of guests. Keep the tone light and inviting, unthreatening. Otherwise, you just might be left with last-minute cancellations or "no-shows."

Another option is to post the house rules in each room, but do this only if major points have been spelled out *before* reservations were secured. Nobody likes surprises, particularly tired travelers arriving late at night.

Ideas you might incorporate in either a "Dear Guest" letter (see sample at end of this chapter) or a house rules list (or both) include:

- ☐ Arrival time.

- ☐ Departure time.

- ☐ Breakfast hours and place(s) of serving.

- ☐ Smoking area(s), if any.

- ☐ Drinking restrictions.

- ☐ Ages of children accepted (if at all).

- ☐ Will you allow pets and under what specific conditions?

- ☐ Indicate pets in your home. Many travelers have allergies.

- ☐ Breakfast options. If only continental is included, will you serve a full breakfast for a small additional charge?

☐ Policies regarding use of the kitchen and/or refrigerator. Ice facilities.

☐ Pool/spa/hot tub rules.

☐ Use of laundry facilities?

☐ If TV or radio is provided in guest rooms, time restrictions (if any).

☐ Lockup time (if any) and house key information.

☐ The degree of maid service to be provided. (See "What, No Maid Service?" section, below.)

☐ Telephone use. Location. Restrictions. Log for recording calls? Method of payment. (See "Guest Use of the Telephone" section, below.)

☐ Parking information.

These are meant to be suggestions only. Choose those that are important. Too many rules only make people uncomfortable and could frighten away guests.

What, No Maid Service?

Each Bed & Breakfast experience is unique. Individual hosts and inns set their rules, planning B&B services around the rest of their busy lives. The working hostess is going to have far less time available for pampering guests than the full-time homemaker or retired couple. Then, too, some hosts may find demeaning the very chore another delights in doing.

As a result, and so there will be no misunderstanding, housekeeping rules should be carefully spelled out. Some inns and Homestays have a tented card on the dresser indicating how often rooms will be cleaned, beds changed, new towels provided, etc. Some send a letter or copy of house rules in advance of arrival. Others simply have the room beautifully prepared, with extra linens in the closet, and tell all new arrivals that, until their departure, guests can be assured that nobody will enter the room except to change sheets on the third (host's option) day. Along with assuring privacy, this subtly lets the traveler know the house offers no daily maid service. Commercial B&B inns operate more like hotels in this area, and even go so far as to turn down beds at night, place a mint on the pillow, or (as in the case at the Willows in San Francisco) place a tray with two glasses and a decanter of cognac on the bed along with a card wishing the guest a pleasant night's sleep.

I treat guests as distant members of the family. In that way, they will accept a certain amount of self-service, and understand sudden necessary shifts in policy. I opt to provide a "Dear Guest" letter in the room, as part of a "packet" that can go home with the traveler as a souvenir (and as a publicity kit, if it is shown to friends and relatives). This information can be referred to when a guest is confused, concerned, or both.

You may wish to make beds and straighten the room daily as done in more commercial inns. You may instead do as we prefer: never enter the room once guests arrive, except for the pre-scheduled linen change. As a rule, I find guests make their own beds before leaving the room for breakfast. Otherwise, returning home to an unmade bed at the end of the first day, they quickly learn our habits. We always keep a change of linens and extra towels in the bedroom closet for emergency use, along with additional blankets and pillows.

The tone of my "Dear Guest" letter indicates the way things are run: casually. I suggest breakfast dishes be put in the sink. I indicate that one can open the freezer at will for ice cubes. I volunteer refrigerator space (not always a good idea; consider this option carefully), and arrange for self-service should breakfast be eaten after our family members have left for the day. With information like this, who would expect maid service?

Guest Use of the Telephone

B&B guests quickly learn the differences between hotels and Homestays or inns. There is no switchboard; in fact, most rooms have no telephone. Wanting to encourage peace and a complete change of pace, many hosts even eliminate television and radio from the rooms, offering (sometimes) a common room with these facilities.

I encourage guests to use the kitchen phone—with one exception! Business travelers (particularly those in sales) may have clients in the East. Since there is a three-hour time difference between coasts, I plug in a telephone near their bed, for my convenience as much as theirs.

Urge guests to call collect, charge calls to their home phone, or use credit cards. If you allow "regular" calls, keep a telephone log for recording any that will be charged to your bill; guests log in the number called, and the time and date of call. Upon checkout, hosts obtain rate information from the operator and collect the appropriate amount.

We have *never* had a problem with abuse of the phone, nor any surprises on receiving our monthly statement.

Should you be planning to purchase or rent another telephone, I suggest you get Touch-tone service and a Touch-tone phone inasmuch as it is the kind needed for use with Sprint, MCI, and the other AT&T competitors that so many business travelers use. A converter or adapter is available for use with existing phones.

Guests are rarely about the house during the day and few calls will be received for them. When I need to take a message, those little yellow Post-it pads come in handy for sticking a memo on the bedroom door. They leave no marks on wallpaper or paint and are highly visible. It is a good idea to leave a pad and pencil next to the phone for guest convenience (and messages they may take for *you* as well).

Sample Telephone Log
HONOR SYSTEM   *PLEASE RECORD ALL CALLS*

Guest Name: _____

Please record all telephone calls as they are made. Include the area code and telephone number, city, state, and length of call in minutes. We will get charges from the operator, or consult the phone book.

This telephone number is (insert your phone number with area code):

Date	Area Code	Telephone Number	City	Time in Min.	Cost	Tax

Please return this log, along with your house key, on your departure date. You must pay for the phone calls and any other charges due at that time.

Thank you.

Sample Guest Letter

Your house number and street
Your city, state, and zip
Phone: (818) 000-0000
Office: (818) 111-1111

Dear Guests:

Welcome to our home and to Los Angeles. We hope you will enjoy your stay.

The bathroom with tub and shower is across the hall. Guest towels and fresh soap are in your room. If you need more, please let us know.

Breakfast is served in the dining area of the living room or on a tray in your bedroom, as you prefer. Please leave your dishes in the kitchen sink. If we are away from the house when you wish breakfast, help yourself to coffee, juice, and toast/rolls as arranged. Should you wish to keep things in the refrigerator, we'll make room. Ice is in the automatic icemaker tray, on the freezer side.

Our pool is swimmable from May until October. You are welcome to use it after signing the insurance release form. (Please don't take any glass into the pool area. We have plastic cups for that use.)

Our dog is Kiska and he is a love, but he's a watchdog! Introduce yourself to him and to our cats, Fraidy and Cloudy. Ziggy, the parrot, is an occasional visitor. He speaks over 500 words—though never when asked—so don't get discouraged!

A window air conditioner and television for your room are available, as is a clock-radio. Just ask.

The house key is for your use, since we keep the front door locked at all times. The last one home sets the night bolt.

Please keep valuables with you, as our insurance does not cover theft of guest articles. We will not enter your room during your stay, except to change linens on the fourth day. A key to the room is in your door, should you wish to lock it. Though ours is a safe neighborhood by city standards, you can never be too careful.

The release is for insurance purposes. Please sign it on arrival.

If prepayment of room charge has not been made, payment is due on arrival with cash or travelers' check.

A commercial bank, City National, is on the corner of Ventura Boulevard and Whitsett Avenue (four blocks west, four blocks south), as is the bus stop for Hollywood and downtown Los Angeles. Public transportation will take you to Universal Studios tour (about five minutes by bus). Bus schedules, restaurant menus and tour information are in a drawer in your room. Brochures are for your use during your stay, but please leave them for the next guest, and collect things to pass along to others when you are sightseeing. Sharing is what B&B is all about.

Fine restaurants, the Studio City movie theater, and the Queen Mary nightclub (famous for its female impersonators) are all on nearby Ventura Boulevard, as are The Sportsman's Lodge (pickup for Greyline Tours and an excellent dining room), La Serre (one of L.A.'s most glamorous and expensive French restaurants), Pavillon, and Café Hyppo (very charming and reasonably priced French bistros), Seafood Broiler (all fresh fish), Tail of the Cock, Carny's (fabulous, messy chiliburgers), Albion's and Camille's (elegant continental restaurants), and dozens of other choices of almost every type. Most of these can be reached by car within five minutes. You can walk to others.

A large supermarket is on the corner of Ventura Boulevard and Whitsett Avenue, and a small market can be found on Coldwater (four blocks west) and Moorpark (one-half block north). The nearby dairy (on Moorpark at Whitsett) carries a few staple items. A liquor store is next door to the dairy.

The library is across the street from the dairy, on Moorpark and Babcock (three blocks east). Public golf with a putting green is at Whitsett and Valley Spring Lane (two blocks south). A little park with free tennis courts is one block north of Moorpark at Beeman (two blocks east).

Actually, we are centrally located and near just about anything you might wish to see, so just ask.

Here is a local map to help you get around, and a phone log to keep track of any calls you may make on our line. Whatever I have forgotten to tell you is available for the asking.

Please let us know if there is anything else we may do to make your stay in our home a fun one.

Buddy & Wally

P.S. Karen, Lauren, Bill, and Tim are our adult children who come in and out of our lives perpetually. Say "hi" if your paths should cross.

CHAPTER 6

Guest Comfort

The words "Bed & Breakfast" instantly conjure up images of the comforts of a home straight from the pages of *House Beautiful,* presided over by an elegantly coiffed *Vogue* model who graciously offers high tea as the *Gourmet Magazine* recipes appear by magic from the spotless kitchen that was recently featured in *Architectural Digest.* One's every whim has been anticipated and catered to—all this at a cost somewhere between youth hostel and YMCA!

The fact of the matter is that no two B&Bs offer the same thing, aside from a bed and some kind of food in the morning. True, elegance and whimsy are the mark of many commercial inns, and private Homestays have sometimes attempted to emulate some of their more creative aspects, but the individuality and personality of each homeowner is what makes this such a wonderful travel experience. The worst possible thing that could happen would be for us all to turn into clones of what we think to be the "perfect" B&B. Thank goodness for imperfections, for they are exactly what the hotel-wary guest is looking for. The sterile, boringly perfect sameness that one comes to expect from hotel chains is precisely what we can guarantee a B&B is not!

Certain basics are essential for guest comfort. The "extras" are up to you. Be imaginative, but true to your own sense of style. This is still your family's home. The majority of my guests make their own beds and clear their dishes instinctively—we have made them

feel "at home." Real people live here and real people are going to visit. Treat them as personal friends and your guests will behave in kind. *A general reminder is in order to all hosts:* Guests choose to stay with us for the warmth, friendliness, and comfort we provide. I underscore the word *comfort* for that is, above all, what we stress. The most beautiful home will not necessarily become a favorite. A touch-me-not quality will turn people away just as rapidly as a messy house. If we can provide the sense of home away from home, we will fulfill what I believe is a major need for many travelers. Those seeking luxury will not come to us in the first place. Those in need of tremendous privacy will stay away as well. Those left are the clients of our future.

Bedroom Essentials

☐ Queen or king-sized bed or twins. (Think twice before investing in a new *double* bed. Travelers often resist this option.)

☐ Extra set of sheets and pillowcases for each bed (i.e., two sets).

☐ Two pillows for each bed (a variety of sizes and firmness is preferable).

☐ Extra quilts or blankets for each bed.

☐ At least one dresser, preferably completely empty, with drawers lined.

☐ Mirror over dresser.

☐ A full-length mirror in room, if possible.

☐ Nightstands on either side of bed.

☐ Bedside reading lamp/lamps . . . one on either side of large beds.

☐ Room-darkening shades or shutters at windows.

☐ Remove all personal possessions from closet, if possible. Otherwise, block off a section. Top shelves may be retained for family "dead" storage.

☐ A large supply of hangers.

☐ Two sets of towels and washcloths for each guest (different colors for each room).

☐ Drinking glass for each guest.

☐ Wrapped soap for each guest, if liquid soap is not provided in the bathroom.

☐ If phone is in room, a notepad and pen.

☐ Ashtrays, if you allow smoking in the room.

☐ Wastebasket.

☐ Table area, if breakfast is to be served in room. This can double as a desk.

☐ Comfortable chair.

☐ Air conditioning or fan for summer months, if needed.

☐ Access to heat controls.

☐ Key, if bedroom door is to be locked.

☐ Front-door key on keychain (large and heavy keychains are best, since they can deter accidental removal on departure day).

☐ Current restaurant menus, tourist information.

☐ Smoke alarm in bedroom hallways.

☐ Radio or television (or both).

☐ Alarm clock.

☐ Quiet. Many travelers are fighting jet lag and tourist fatigue. Bedrooms should be usable at any hour for sleeping.

☐ Welcome packet or letter, if not sent with confirmation.

Play guest in your own home. Spend a night in each room before opening for business. You will know soon enough if sufficient reading light is near the bed, if curtains look fresh, if a comfortable spot for writing is provided. Evaluate each potential guest area as if you are paying the bill.

Sample Guest Packet

Presented on arrival, or left in the guest room, a package of pertinent information, enclosed in a colorful binder or clear acetate
folder, might include:

● "Dear Guest" welcome letter. See previous chapter.

● A neighborhood map with host's location marked in red. Host
name, address, and phone number should be prominently displayed on
the map, along with work telephone numbers. Nearby points of interest, public transportation stops, parks, banks, etc. could be pointed
out, along with nearest freeway exits. This same map might be included with confirmation of reservation.

● City Map.

● Breakfast menu (see page 81).

● Tea service order, patterned after the breakfast menu (see
page 81).

● Höuse rules, if not in "Dear Guest" letter (see page 56 for ideas).

● B&B brochure for souvenir (see page 111).

● Letterhead stationery, postcards, envelopes.

● Insurance release form (see page 36).

● Telephone log (see page 59).

● Services provided (see page 57).

● Optional services available at extra cost.

● Request for guest comments to be left on departure.

Bedroom Extras

B&B guests come to expect surprises. The little touches that per-
sonalize our homes are the things most remembered—long after
house rules are forgotten. Here are a few suggestions that may or
may not appeal to you. Discard what you like, but do attempt to
find a few extra touches to enhance your special style. Travelers

will talk about the generosity of your hospitality and the word will spread (the best kind of promotion).

- Freshly baked cookies at bedside in the evening.

- Soft flannel nightshirts, as at Smithton in Ephrata, Pennsylvania.

- Extra-large square down pillows, again as at Smithton.

- Guest book for signing, with space for comments.

- Baskets of sample-size goodies in room: sun screen, suntan lotion, special soaps, shampoo and conditioner, disposable shower caps.

- Jar of wrapped candies in room.

- Decanter of sherry with glasses in bedroom.

- Oversized or beach towels if you have a pool or are near water activities.

- Oversized terry robes in closet for rooms that must share the bath. Good also for pool use.

- Fresh fruit bowl in room.

- Sachet in closets and/or drawers.

- Padded, scented coat hangers.

- An assortment of books on many topics for varied reading tastes.

- Travel and B&B-related material. An exchange of brochures between B&Bs would be good promotion for one another, and makes interesting reading.

- Fresh flowers, a single flower in bud vase, or plants in the bedroom. Lovely silk flower arrangements will cost less than fresh over the long term, but there is something special about "fresh."

- Mending supplies.

- Iron and ironing board.

- Electric blanket (on every bed at Country House Inn, Templeton, California).

- Writing supplies. If you have letterhead or personalized postcards, this is another way to get direct-mail promotion through referral.

- Luggage rack, or alternative, for holding suitcases.

• At checkout, a small gift (homemade craft item, or a loaf of your special bread, as at The Colonel Ebenezer Crafts Inn, Old Sturbridge, Massachusetts.

• Specially crafted giant-sized coffee mugs (that guests can fill and take back to bed as in rooms at Cedar Street Place, Calistoga, California).

Bathroom Essentials

☐ A large-capacity hot-water heater. Installation of a new one, if needed, is relatively inexpensive compared to the loss of guests after an unwanted cold shower!

☐ Several rolls of bath tissue.

☐ Liquid soap in a container at both tub and sink. (A soap dish could be placed in each room instead.)

☐ Non-skid bath mats and rugs.

☐ Disposable paper bath mats or rubber tub-and-shower mat.

☐ Medicine cabinet.

☐ Mirror.

☐ Bathroom lock.

☐ Wastebasket. Plastic or paper-bag linings are easy to replace, but not very aesthetic looking.

☐ Directions for heater/fan/light use.

☐ Night light on twenty-four hours when guests are present.

☐ Scouring powder, sponge, tub/sink cleanser, long-handled tub brush, bowl cleaner.

☐ Bathroom deodorizers.

☐ No family items in a private bath. Ideally, the bath is for guest use only, but if family members must share, have a specific, separate area for family belongings.

Sharing the Bath

Though more and more inns are creating private baths to accommodate the demands of most American travelers, older buildings and private homes simply lack adequate plumbing and/or sufficient space to create new baths. Sometimes hosts will not have the tremendous amount of funds needed to do costly remodeling. Thus, shared baths, particularly in less expensive establishments, are a common occurrence. Coping with potential problems before the fact will alleviate most and minimize others. Take a few minutes to examine the list below and check off pertinent items as they are handled. Cross out whatever does not apply to your situation.

Shared-Bath Checklist

☐ Sufficient towel racks for each room, or towel rack *in* each room.

☐ Guest name or room name above towel racks in bathroom.

☐ Different-colored towels for each room.

☐ Lots of bath tissue.

☐ Disposable seat covers.

☐ Long-handled baskets (lined to coordinate with room fabrics?) to carry bathroom supplies from bedroom to bath and back.

☐ Tub-cleaning equipment in sight (to remind guests to clean up after themselves).

☐ Check baths several times daily.

☐ Disposable paper slippers (like the ones used in hospitals).

☐ Robes for guest use. Some inns (the Willows, San Francisco) have their logo inscribed on robes, and sell new versions as mementos.

☐ "Occupied" signs on all doors to alleviate constant knocking.

☐ Well-oiled doors that close quietly. I spent one unforgettable night in a B&B listening to the door opening and closing in the bath across the hall.

☐ Make plumbing as noiseless as possible for the comfort of all.

When family members simply must share with guests, it is important to remove personal items immediately after use. Always give bath priority to guests, even if this necessitates a change of shower habits. Most B&B travelers leave early in the morning and retire early. Few stay around the house during the day. By adjusting to their schedules, you will also lessen the possibility of running out of hot water.

Bathroom Extras That Could Be Included in Either Private or Shared Facilities

- Bath beads or water softeners for tub.

- Cologne and after-shave lotion.

- Emergency items: bandages, cotton, adhesive tape, Band-Aids, mercurochrome, cotton swabs, aspirin, rubbing alcohol.

- Safety railings in shower, etc., for disabled.

- Electrical outlets at sink.

- European-style heated towel racks, as in the Westlane Inn, Ridgefield, Connecticut.

- Hair dryer.

Major Guest Complaints Regarding Bathrooms

The most common complaint from guests seems to be the lack of care paid to the bath. This room must shine.

☐ Check grout in tiles for mildew.

☐ Is the shower floor clean?

☐ Do drains work well?

☐ Shower curtains should be stain-free. Replace them if they're not. Clear plastic linings are reasonably inexpensive and are easy to clean.

☐ Ring around the bathtub? Water softener often helps.

☐ Check faucet screens for mineral buildup, often the cause of reduced water flow.

☐ Dripping faucets?

☐ Running toilet?

☐ A hard-water mark in the toilet bowl? An automatic bowl cleaner is an absolute must.

☐ Keep mirrors and tile sparkling with window cleaner.

☐ Finger marks on the light switches or woodwork?

If you were a stranger walking into this bathroom for the first time, would it look sterile and safe to use? Look again. Look one more time.

Breakfast

Breakfast is a very important part of B&B. Guests anticipate this social time with the host and other guests. Some B&Bs provide a continental breakfast. Others offer a larger "extended" continental or even a full American breakfast. Whatever your preference, I think it should be included in the total lodging price. To charge additionally for the slightly larger meal is pennywise, to my way of thinking. Some working hosts serve a continental breakfast during the week, and splurge with a bountiful buffet on Saturday and Sunday. This works exceptionally well for business guests who are out and about early on weekdays.

In our home, breakfast varies with our current activity. Should I be working, the dining table is set up the night before, single-serving cold cereals are put in a basket, coffee is ready to turn on in the electric pot, juice and a pitcher of milk sit ready in the refrigerator, muffins or other easily prepared rolls are in foil waiting to be warmed, cheese is placed out just before I leave, and I'm on my way. Naturally, guests have been alerted to my schedule the night before.

On the other hand, if one of us will be around, we prepare food as selected from our "menu" (see page 81) and serve it in the dining area or bedroom, as the guests wish. Most of the time we find ourselves sitting with them.

There are those times when guests will leave at an outrageously early hour. Most people with early plane schedules prefer to dash off without food, occasionally refusing even coffee. Concerned with traffic congestion and the possibility of missing a flight, they want to get luggage checked and boarding pass in hand before

relaxing in the airport coffee shop. In this case, food is set out as if we will not be home, and we say a fond farewell the night before, sleeping on as they run to catch the plane. It all works out.

Do what works best for you and your lifestyle. If a family member has time and enjoys preparing meals, by all means, offer a large breakfast. The cost is only nominally more, and your reputation for generosity will undoubtedly return home with the traveler. However, if yours is an active, involved family rushing out early in the day, time spent cooking and serving might put a strain on everyone. If that is the case, serve what is easiest for you, but do it with style and sizeable portions. In that way, nobody feels cheated.

Simple Menu Ideas

Whatever the hour of breakfast, present a selection of easily prepared dishes that have good staying power on the table (for that inevitable latecomer).

- Flaky croissants, plain or filled with fruit, ham, cheese, mushrooms, spinach, or a combination of ingredients.

- Cinnamon toast.

- Bagels (with cream cheese, lox, chives, etc.).

- Scones.

- Strawberry shortcake.

- Muffins (infinite variety here!).

- Freshly baked yeast bread.

- Cinnamon rolls.

- Philadelphia sticky buns.

- Corn sticks or corn bread.

- Fruit breads of all seasons (persimmon, apple, cranberry, lemon).

- Fresh fruit (often picked by guests from the yard).

- Freshly squeezed juices, topped with banana slices or berries.

- Fruit compote.

- Boiled eggs, individually served in their own twig baskets, as at The Glendeven Inn, Little River, California.

- Specially ground coffee. Some inns package and sell their private label, a good mail-order item.

- Variety of choices in both regular and herb teas.

- Unusual jams and jellies. These can be sold, too.

- Unique syrups. Port wine syrup is served at the Magnolia Hotel, Yountville, California.

- Grand Marnier French toast is served at Johnson House in Florence, Oregon.

- Bread pudding.

- Gingerbread.

- Popovers.

- Strudel.

- Breakfast "cookies."

- English muffins.

- Pancakes with pecans, blueberries or cinnamon apples, as served at Grane's Fairhaven Inn, Bath, Maine.

- Fresh berries with cream or crème fraîche.

- Baked apples and stuffed pears, as served at the Pride House in Jefferson, Texas.

- Spiced hamballs à la Middletown Springs Inn in Vermont.

- Raspberry sauce made from fresh-picked berries and served over pancakes, as it is at Barley Sheaf Farm, Holicong, Pennsylvania.

- Orange-apricot Grand Marnier whipped butter is on the French toast at The Inn, Stockbridge, Massachusetts.

- Full, elaborate vegetarian breakfasts are served at The Turning Point in Great Barrington, Massachusetts.

- Full English-style breakfast of kippers, grilled tomato, sautéed chicken livers, and more is part of the breakfast menu at the 1811 House, Manchester Center, Vermont.

- Homemade sausage and hand-ground grain for bread are a specialty of the hostess at Bayview House, Morrow Bay, California.

- Plain yogurt with choice of fruit sauces, nuts, raisins, other garnishes.

● Selections of Melba toast, Holland rusk, assorted crackers, served with:

● A choice of mini-cheeses, cheese spreads, variety of cheese slices.

● Homemade granola.

● Individually packaged cereals.

● Beverages might include, in addition to the usual coffee, tea and decaffeinated coffee:

  ● Assorted herb teas or decaffeinated tea.

  ● Assorted exotic teas.

  ● Flavored coffees: cinnamon, orange, mint, etc.

  ● Ovaltine. La Maida House, North Hollywood, California, offers Ovaltine as a bedtime option.

  ● Cocoa.

  ● Hot soup or broth. A particularly good choice in the winter.

  ● Cold summer soups, particularly fruit and berry.

In researching menu ideas, ethnic recipe books offer wonderful suggestions. Scandinavian breads and soups, Middle Eastern dips such as hummous and tahini, French and Italian breads and pastries, Irish soda breads, Scottish and English biscuits and scones, English lemon curd—the ideas are endless! Local libraries have immense cookbook selections for additional ideas, and several cookbooks are on the market with collections of recipes from inns.

Breakfast Time

● When the gong sounds at Sutter Creek Inn, Sutter, California at nine A.M. sharp, a huge breakfast is served. Latecomers miss out!

● Music from a computerized player piano announces breakfast at The Manor House, Cape May, New Jersey.

● A full breakfast is served from dawn until nine-thirty A.M. at Baker's Bed & Breakfast in Stone Ridge, New York.

● Breakfast is served in the book-lined library room at The Inn at Rancho Santa Fe, California.

- At the Woolverton Inn, Stockton, New Jersey, guests may have breakfast at any time of the day and wherever they choose to eat.

- Guests walk through the garden to the reception room at the Vagabond House Inn, Carmel, California. Breakfast, served on a tray, can be eaten on the patio or in the bedroom.

- Specify the time, and a thermos of tea or coffee will be placed in a basket outside your door in the morning at the Prince of Wales Inn, Baltimore, Maryland.

- A hot thermos of tea or coffee will be brought to your door before breakfast at 29 South Cedar in Lititz, Pennsylvania.

- Murphy's Inn, Grass Valley, California, has a call button in each room. When the button is pressed, breakfast arrives on a tray.

- Country breakfast is served in the dining room at a set time and continental breakfast is brought to your room earlier at the Manor Farm Inn, Poulsbo, Washington.

- Special diets are accommodated with advance notice at Pineapple Hill, New Hope, Pennsylvania.

- At a prearranged time, breakfast is delivered in a basket to each room in the cottage and main house of the Glenborough Inn, Santa Barbara, California.

- Breakfast is served in the greenhouse at the Valerio Manor in Santa Barbara.

- You'll eat breakfast in front of the fire in the living/dining room at the Chateau Victorian, Santa Cruz, California, after serving yourself from a beautiful buffet.

- Have breakfast delivered on a tray to your room or served in the sitting room at The Willows in San Francisco.

Other breakfast areas commercial inns have used include tree-covered decks, gardens, terraces and patios, buffet-style in outdoor latticed areas, at long English harvest tables (great for guest interaction). Other hosts simply announce that breakfast is for the taking "anywhere."

Most B&Bs specify a time for serving breakfast—generally between eight-thirty and nine-thirty A.M., unless otherwise requested by the guest.

You may wish to utilize a check-off menu that is set out each day (see menu sample, below, for an example of a "check-off" style menu). I like this method since it gives both host and guest leeway to change options without a lengthy discussion. Knowing that we are rarely home at the same time except to sleep, it is far easier to rely on a written system.

Another option is to set up a buffet table for a period of several hours, leaving guests to wander in and out at will. Though this appears to be less confining, I have found it to be quite a nuisance. One worries about a coffeepot left on too long, food drying out, juice getting warm. Thus, the tendency is to stay available (and annoyed) while waiting for the last straggler to finally arrive.

Some B&Bs will have coffee made and available in the kitchen at a very early hour; guests are free to help themselves. A full breakfast will then be served later.

Food Presentation Ideas

To some, presentation is as important as the meal itself. Presentation ideas can be gleaned from gourmet cooking magazines, particularly around holiday seasons. Why not keep a clipping file of serving suggestions such as:

● Individually packaged cold cereals in a basket with colorful napkin lining to match table linens.

● An assortment of cheeses (or slices) under a glass cheese dome, separated by grapes, pineapple wedges, or other fruit slices.

● Napkins in holders with a garden flower tucked inside.

● Hard-boiled eggs dyed in Easter egg colors—all year long.

● Generous use of paper doilies on serving plates.

● Unusual serving pieces: Antique tins to hold Sweet-n-Low. Brown sugar in earthenware jars. Milk and cream in antique miniature milk bottles. Softened butter and margarine in individual mini-pots.

● Soufflés can be frozen (precooked or uncooked) in individual serving dishes and served right from the oven.

● A selection of jams look colorful in long stemware, particularly wineglass shapes.

Sample Menus

Continental Breakfast

PLEASE COMPLETE AND LEAVE ON THE HALL TABLE
OUTSIDE YOUR ROOM. THANK YOU.

DATE: _____

WE WOULD LIKE BREAKFAST AT 8:30 ☐
9:00 ☐
9:30 ☐

PLEASE SERVE IN OUR ROOM ☐   ON PATIO ☐
DINING AREA ☐

JUICE: ORANGE ☐   APPLE ☐   V-8 ☐   TOMATO ☐

BREAD: TOAST: WHITE ☐   or WHEAT ☐   or ROLLS ☐
or ENGLISH MUFFIN ☐   or FRENCH BREAD ☐

CONDIMENTS: BUTTER ☐   MARGARINE ☐
HONEY ☐   JAM ☐

BEVERAGES: COFFEE ☐   SANKA ☐   TEA ☐   HERB
TEA ☐   MILK ☐

EXTRAS: CREAM ☐   LEMON ☐   SUGAR ☐
SUGAR SUBSTITUTE ☐

GUEST NAME: _____

ROOM: _____

Extended Continental Breakfast

PLEASE COMPLETE AND LEAVE ON THE HALL TABLE
OUTSIDE YOUR ROOM. THANK YOU.

DATE: _____

WE WOULD LIKE BREAKFAST AT 8:30 ☐
9:00 ☐
9:30 ☐

PLEASE SERVE IN OUR ROOM ☐   ON PATIO ☐
IN DINING ROOM ☐

JUICE: ORANGE ☐   APPLE ☐   V-8 ☐   TOMATO ☐
FRESH FRUIT (SEASONAL) ☐

BREAD: TOAST: WHITE ☐   or WHEAT ☐
or ROLLS ☐

or ENGLISH MUFFIN ☐   *or* FRENCH BREAD ☐

CONDIMENTS: BUTTER ☐   MARGARINE ☐
HONEY ☐   JAM ☐   CHEESE ☐

CEREAL: COLD CEREAL ☐   MILK ☐   SUGAR ☐
BEVERAGES: COFFEE ☐   SANKA ☐   TEA ☐
HERB TEA ☐   MILK ☐

EXTRAS: CREAM ☐   LEMON ☐   SUGAR ☐
SUGAR SUBSTITUTE ☐

GUEST NAME: _____

ROOM: _____

Extra Meals

Serving additional meals can be an excellent way to provide a much-wanted service while earning extra dollars. Since continental breakfast is included in all B&B, an extended or full breakfast could be served as an optional extra. Some owners provide this as part of the room charge, but whatever your choice make certain potential guests are fully aware of exactly what is included in that second "B" prior to check-in. Nobody likes surprises where money is involved.

If you enjoy cooking and plan to offer additional meals to your guests, I suggest you pick a specialty, create a menu or two, and place a tent card on the dresser or a descriptive insert in the guest packet that will be sent along with room confirmation or given on arrival.

In the case of snacks, tea, box lunches, and any other food offerings to be purchased, be quite specific about the selections and costs.

Many cities have stringent rulings about how and where food "for sale" is to be prepared. Make certain to carefully check the laws if they exist in your area. If it is impossible to serve a cooked meal for a fee in your area without doing expensive kitchen remodeling or buying commercial equipment (special fans, dishwashers, vents, sinks, etc.), you might consider arranging with a small baker or caterer to provide meals precooked in his or her approved and inspected facility. Many B&B inns use this means to avoid the costly and often quite arbitrary rulings set down by local Boards of Health. Another option is to provide all cold foods.

If your codes are so extreme as to prevent even home baking, you can consider renting a kitchen at a school, church or community center, or even a restaurant during hours when it is closed. You can do considerable cooking and baking in a few short hours, sealing and freezing food for later use. In the case of religious or school groups, you might even arrange a barter system, giving a donation of food to the next fund-raiser or bazaar in exchange for occasional use of kitchen facilities.

As foolish as some laws might seem, the important thing is to protect yourself from any possibility of legal action as a result of this or any business endeavor. Travel in and of itself can create stomach disorders simply from the constant change of water, altitude, and constant sitting. An ill guest may truly believe that the meal you prepared caused his/her problems, while in fact the change of temperatures brought on the symptoms. Again, I must stress that you be prepared for all possibilities, no matter how remote.

I myself have simply taken the easiest route. We do not offer any hot meals, much as I enjoy cooking.

If you want to serve extra meals, consider:

- Late-night snacks for guests arriving from long distances (some hosts provide this service free of charge).

- Box or picnic lunch for a day trip or on departure day. Ingredients may be simple or gourmet fare. Whatever the menu, it is bound to be more interesting than the food found in stops along a freeway route. The time-saving element is important as well. If you mimic the fare of chic take-out establishments, you can often command top prices.

- A specialty dinner. Your grandmother's secret *moussaka* recipe, your special chicken dish, or a fancier standing rib roast can all be offered.

- Nutritious "snack packs" for kids (granola, dried fruit, juice) might appeal to health-conscious parents.

- An inexpensive but delightful touch to offer guests is afternoon tea or wine. Few visitors are home at that hour, but if they are, this little extra will be a pleasant prelude to an evening out, or the calming end to a hectic day.

Some hosts set a regular time for the late-day offering. Others simply suggest it whenever guests return to change for dinner.

When travelers arrive at our home, generally in the late afternoon, we always offer them something to drink, serving in front of the fire during the winter, and on the patio in the summer.

A tray might be put on a table in the guest room or living room, available at will. However, if edibles other than peanuts or some such easily stored item are provided, time limits are essential to maintain freshness.

An invitation to tea and snacks, or wine and appetizers, could be left in the bedroom or in the guest packet.

Tea or snacks are extra details that make the B&B stay a special one. Teatime often provides host and guest a chance to relax together. The cost is minimal, but the payoff is big.

What the Big Guys Do to Make Guests Feel Special

- Kay Mattos of Sisson 1904, Mount Shasta, California, will give you the recipe for her homemade raspberry cordial if you ask.

- Hors d'oeuvres and sherry are served by the fireplace at The Manor Farm Inn in Poulsbo, Washington.

- Cordials, tea, and cookies in the early evening, and warm cookies and milk at bedtime are the hallmarks of The Jabberwock, Monterey, California.

- Plum wine and fortune cookies are served in the Madame Butterfly room of the Fay Mansion, San Francisco.

- When returning to The Willows, San Francisco, guests find the bed covers turned back, candy on the pillow, a tray with brandy-filled glasses and a card wishing guests a good night.

- A decanter of Napa Valley wine is in each room at Burgundy House and the Magnolia Hotel, both in Yountville, California.

- Homemade cheeses and California sherry are served at the Old Monterey Inn, California.

- High tea is served every afternoon at The Montecito Inn, Santa Barbara, California.

- Cognac is placed next to the bed of suite guests at El Encanto Hotel in Santa Barbara.

- The Willows inserts a tea menu in their guest packet offering this option at an extra cost of $1.50.

- Teatime is four P.M. every day at Clefstone Manor, Bar Harbor, Maine, when scones and shortbread are served at a massive dining table.

- Exercise, relaxation, and stress therapy programs are offered at Ujjala's Bed and Breakfast, New Paltz, New York.

- Lap blankets, chairs, and ashtrays are on the veranda of The Gingerbread Mansion, Ferndale, California.

- Weekday limousine service to downtown is provided by the Queen Anne in San Francisco.

- A sachet of potpourri is on each pillow at The Mansion, San Francisco.

- Complimentary daily newspapers are delivered with breakfast at many B&Bs. If not brought to rooms, they should be available in the dining room or common rooms.

- L'Ermitage in Beverly Hills includes with its bed turn-down service a late-night snack of fresh strawberries with cream and brown sugar.

- At the Casa Madrona, Sausalito, California, an "artist's loft" bedroom contains paints, brushes and easel.

- Late-night arrivals receive a biscuit and a cup of hot chocolate at The Marshlands, New Brunswick, Canada.

- Heritage House, in Little River, California, has an album with photos of each room so guests may choose from those available.

- Some B&Bs provide an indoor toy box and children's library/play area.

- Others do an overnight shoeshine, when shoes are left outside the room.

- Boots and umbrellas on a hall tree for dreary days are provided at several B&Bs.

- Wheelchair access is always a plus.

- Some B&B hosts treat guests to a sleigh ride or a boat ride.

Attitude

I cannot stress strongly enough the importance of attitude on the part of family members participating in B&B. We have all had good and bad restaurant encounters, leaving the bad ones with the exclamation, "Never again!" Pity the prepaid B&B guest who is forced to tolerate another day (or lose money by leaving early) under less-than-happy conditions. Unfortunately, neither price, location, or "hype" can guarantee a satisfying stay. As a host, the way you talk to guests, serve meals, and meet challenges can mean the difference between a wonderful vacation and a mediocre one.

I recently had a very bad experience at a highly touted (and highly priced) B&B in San Francisco. Breakfast was served in an enormous sitting room. Physical comfort was everywhere. However, the toaster-oven set out for guests to heat their own croissants (with a penciled note on the wall above advising that a second helping would cost one dollar), did much to diminish whatever charm we had first seen. To add to the tackiness of the situation, some guests were left totally unattended while others were hovered over. Second cups of coffee were offered to only the select few. I found myself seated with first-time B&B travelers, and spent the entire breakfast assuring them that this was atypical and to give B&B another try. Obviously, the old adage "service with a smile" is not just another platitude. We have also learned the hard way that a charming host can make up for a lack in creature comforts.

Common Areas

In order to guarantee sanity among regular family members and to give some semblance of privacy to guests, definite boundaries must be established. Family quarters should be as far away from guest rooms as possible to lessen the feeling of invasion. Guest rooms should be in a quiet zone, buffered from regular family activity, neighborhood noises, and other distractions that might disturb the sleep of exhausted travelers.

On the other hand, common areas must be available to avoid the cooped-up feeling travelers get from most motels and the average hotel. Warmth and openness are trademarks of B&B, and the common areas are where graciousness is best shown.

The living room is the hub of B&B activity. Studies and dens might serve as additional "free" space. Dining areas and other serving bases are natural spots for conversation at mealtime, and table setup should encourage intermingling. Ideas to help create warmth in the common areas:

- A selection of sherry, burgundy, and zinfandel on a sideboard or cabinet, along with a supply of wineglasses.

- Board games, playing cards, bridge scorecards.

- Dart board/darts.

- Piano and sheet music. Player pianos are great ice breakers, as are guitars, harmonicas, and other musical instruments.

- Copies of Bed and Breakfast books for other areas of the country.

● Bound photo album of former guests. Polaroids are taken for both the album and as souvenirs for the traveler.

● A three-ring binder with acetate sheets protecting menus of area restaurants. Former guests' comments, in-house "critiques" would be fun reading.

● A scrapbook of tourist activities and historical information about the vicinity.

● A well-stocked library (with "return to library" request on inside cover) covering a multitude of interests. Library used-book sales and local garage sales are a fine source of recent fiction.

● Exercise room with stationary bike, rowing machine, small weights, jump rope.

● Pool or billiard table.

● Tape deck with tapes, stereo with albums, cassette recorder with cassettes. AM-FM radio.

● If a TV is considered, this would be the area of choice in which to place it.

Outdoor Common Areas and Equipment

Suggestions for outdoor use of common areas include:

● Hammock (under a tree, naturally).

● Swimming pool with pool toys, life jackets, posted rules.

● Sandbox.

● Porch swing.

● Children's swing set.

● Hot tub.

● Spa.

● Tree house. Some inns allow overnight sleeping above.

● Croquet, badminton, shuffleboard equipment.

● Roller and ice skates.

● Tricycles, bikes, tandems.

- Sleds.

- Snowshoes.

- Ski equipment for downhill and cross-country.

- Water sports items, if near ocean, streams, etc.:
  - Fishing equipment.
  - Snorkel and scuba gear.
  - Canoes, rafts, sailboats.
  - Beach umbrella.
  - Surfing and water-ski needs.

- Horseshoes for pitching.

- Ping-Pong table, indoors or out.

- Volley ball equipment.

When considering some of the above, remember that guidelines and instructions are helpful to the guest, as well as accident protection for you.

Do You Think You Need More Room?

If you feel your home lacks enough space for B&Bing, before getting into extensive remodeling, be certain to carefully check out the hidden, unused (or inadequately used) inside footage before proceeding to expand. It is amazing to see how much wasted space there is within an existing structure. Refer to decorating books and magazines such as *House Beautiful, Architectural Digest, Apartment Living, Sunset, House & Garden,* and explore your library bookshelves.

Speak with contractors before remodeling. Get several estimates. Remember that permits are necessary, inspections must pass local building codes, and your taxes may change if major changes are made. Again, I suggest you look once more at the existing house before adding new rooms.

- A high-ceilinged room might be ideal for creating a loft library or sleeping alcove.

- Could an extra-large bedroom hold sleeping for three (a queen-sized bed and a single; a pair of twin beds with trundle bed under one)?

- Could a long hallway be divided into extra bath space?

- Could a long hallway with bedroom and bath on opposite sides become a larger bedroom and connecting bath by removing the hall wall on the bedroom side?

- Could under-stairwell storage be created?

- What about a powder room under the stairs?

- Can a patio or terrace be enclosed to become a garden room/eating area?

- An attached greenhouse creates a beautiful setting for dining.

- Can the area between your house and garage become a useful part of the house?

- Large baths may be split to create two.

- If bath plumbing is against a closet wall, the closet is a relatively inexpensive bath conversion possibility.

- Convert an existing room closet into a private bath. Furnish the room with an armoire to provide hanging space. This is an attractive and common sight in many of the most luxurious inns.

- Living areas might be created by enclosing part of the front porch.

- Attached garages open up a wealth of remodeling space.

- Keep looking!

When the Walls Won't Move: Out-of-the-House Possibilities

If all creative ideas within the existing structure have been exhausted, and you don't want to add on, consider these expansion ideas from other B&Bs:

- The Gazebo is a converted children's playhouse at MacCallum House in Mendocino, California.

- The Howard Creek Ranch, Westport, California, converted a boathouse and a cabin; both have woodstoves and are quite primitive.

- A Homestay in Philadelphia created a bedroom from the potting shed, with the bath formed from the attached greenhouse.

- An adjoining rustic barn was put to use at English Meadows Inn, Kennebunkport, Maine.

- Units were created from the summer kitchen and a smokehouse at Merrell Tavern Inn, South Lee, Massachusetts.

- A two-story converted barn at Cornell House, Lenox, Massachusetts, provides extra space.

- The Brinley Victorian Inn of Newport, Rhode Island, consists of two houses connected by a walkway.

- A creekside cabin provides special away-from-it-all privacy at the Rynders' in B&B in Pescadero, California.

- The Old Milano Hotel of Gualala, California, has created a suite from an old caboose.

- Madrona Manor in Healdsburg, California, used an adjacent carriage house for more space.

- A tree house at the Shadow Mountain Ranch in Julian, California, offers sleeping under the stars, with two levels of privacy.

- Garrets, water towers, stables, greenhouses, wash sheds, miners' cabins, and even cellars could and have been adapted.

Decorating Your B&B

It is important for future hosts to understand that one need not own a historic home, collect period furniture, or have a degree in interior decorating to create a warm, hospitable, successful B&B. Contemporary furnishings are acceptable and even preferred by many guests. Eclectic (a bit of everything) is quite chic these days, and—in my opinion—discloses the personality of the homeowner best. When I suggest you look at decorating and design ideas, this is meant strictly as a guideline for getting your own creative juices flowing, and to provide clues for specific problem solving. The most important ingredient in your home is you, and no other person can get inside your skin.

The entire house need not be perfect or finished when the first guest arrives. Curb appeal is important. The common living areas are of concern. Baths rank at the top of the list in updating and decorating. Then start on the first bedroom. After guests begin to arrive and some income is being generated, go on to the next project, fixing up your B&B room-by-room as business increases.

Works in progress can be fun to explore with your guests. Get their suggestions and advice. Make them a part of the ongoing experience. Drop a note to former guests when the next stage of decorating/remodeling is completed. The B&B will have a special meaning to them as a result.

- Old washstands, small dressers, and nightstands can all be converted into in-room sinks, as guests have seen in many commercial inns that lack private baths.

- Claw-foot tubs are charming but, being old, are often in disrepair. If the outside is worn, try wallpapering the sides to match bathroom wallpaper.

- Enclose a television set in a Victorian cabinet if it upsets the room's look. Modern conveniences can jar an antique feeling.

- Disguise ugly plumbing fixtures beneath sinks with boxed cabinets. Louvered shutters make good doors, with the shutter look repeated on cabinets. This same effect is beautiful for replacing kitchen cupboard fronts.

- Too little closet space can be remedied with a bentwood hatstand, "antique" brass hooks installed on an oak board and mounted either on a wall or inside the door, or with series of baskets hanging in an interesting design.

- Too little room for a large dining table? Use several small ice cream-style tables for four, or a few unmatched tables "matched" with long-skirted cloths. Flat sheets make good material for these table skirts, since they are wide enough to allow you to cut a large circle—without seams. Fabric left over after cutting can be used for matching napkins (either dinner or cocktail size) and/or to cover seats of small dining chairs. Small strips of the remnants, used as tiebacks for curtains, will bring the entire eating area into a coordinated look. White-sale shopping for king-sized sheets to start this project is just one example of "dimestore decorating."

- Too little wall space? Put a small dresser in the closet. Or, build floor-to-ceiling shelves on one side of the closet.

- Antique headboards can be widened to accommodate modern queen- and king-sized beds. For metal headboards, speak with an ornamental ironworker.

● Short of storage space in the bathroom? Hanging shower caddies are inexpensive. Corner shelves can be hung in bath and shower areas. Wicker plant stands make excellent towel holders as well as space for bath necessities.

Decorating Tips from Commercial Inns

● Teddybears (for sale) frolic everywhere in the Gosby House Inn, Pacific Grove, California.

● Each step on the staircase of Beal House in Littleton, New Hampshire, holds part of a collection of bookends and doorstops, along with books.

● At the Centrella Hotel, Pacific Grove, California, room numbers are placed on tiny patchwork pillows hung on each door.

● A pedal-operated sewing machine is used as a lamp table at the Carriage House in Laguna Beach, California.

● A china chamberpot is at the foot of each bed at the Mine House Inn of Amador City, California.

● A sled-topped coffee table is in the living room of Sutter Creek Inn, Sutter, California.

● Floors, walls, and window shades are stenciled at the Apple Lane Inn, Aptos, California.

● Each room at the Britt House, San Diego, California, has its own stuffed mascot.

● A dried wreath hangs on the door of each room at Chestnut Hill in Milford, New Jersey.

● In keeping with its history, the wine chest in the Old Yacht Club Inn of Santa Barbara, California, was formerly a ship's wardrobe.

● The Bear Flag Inn owner collects flags, flying them one by one from the porch of his Sacramento, California, location.

● The Tom Mix Suite of the Mount View Hotel, Calistoga, California, has furniture made from steer horns and a chandelier made of deer antlers.

● The Carole Lombard Suite of the Mount View Hotel, Calistoga, California is decorated in soft pink, with a mirrored headboard and photos of the star.

● The Edgemont Inn of San Diego, California, decorates for Christmas with theme trees in each room. Breakfast is served on Christmas china and silver; holiday drinks are served by the fire.

● A hot-water bottle with cover in fabric to match curtains is in guest rooms at the Priory Country House, Ferndale, California.

● Sheets and towels are color-coordinated with the rooms at numerous inns.

● All furniture in The Willows, San Francisco, is handcrafted from what else?—California gypsy willow.

Sources for Decorating and Remodeling Products for Your B&B

● *Country Notebook*
1633 Renovator's Old Mill
Millers Falls, MA 01349
A catalog of unusual accessories. Cost: $2.00

● *Victorian Homes*
6010 Renovator's Old Mill
Millers Falls, MA 01349
A quarterly magazine with full-color ideas and information on decorating your Victorian home. Cost $12.00/yr.

● *Renovator's Supply*
Millers Falls, MA 01349
Shaker, Victorian to country. Hard-to-find replacement items for remodelers. Catalog: $2.00.

● *The Emporium*
Dept. PH 2515 Morse
Houston, TX 77019
(713) 528-3808
Exclusive sales agent for Anthony Wood Products' handcrafted Victorian gingerbread replicas (corbels, trim, railings, corner brackets, fretwork). Pictorial catalog: $2.00.

● Explore libraries and newsstands for magazines and books that reflect your taste. Read the numerous B&B inn guides that contain magnificent color photographs of B&B interiors. Visit local B&Bs and Homestays for both market and design research. And remember that most of these costs are tax deductible, as long as they are business-related!

CHAPTER 7

Reservations and Checkout

When booking through a reservation service, the RSO serves as the middleman, writing or calling the B&B host with pertinent information about a potential guest. If the dates are convenient and all of the details satisfying to the host, the RSO then requests a deposit from the traveler. Upon receipt, confirmation is returned to the guest with information about the hosts, their home location and amenities, along with the due date for final payment and details of RSO refund rules. Each RSO has its own methods for securing deposits and payment in full. This will be explained by RSOs when you are looking to become affiliated as a member host.

Some RSOs collect the deposit as their commission. Others collect a larger sum, sending the rest to the host, who in turn receives the balance due upon arrival of the traveler. Others collect the entire room fee before guests arrive, turning over the host's portion either in advance of guest arrival or at some specified time of the month. Some RSOs have very simple bookkeeping setups. Others are quite complicated, particularly those who do volume business. When RSOs take care of all the money matters, you can be the genial host without dealing with finances at all unless the visitor stays longer than anticipated. In that case, payment of any extra money due (additional nights, telephone, related services) can be made on the day of departure, or the evening before if a very early leave-taking is anticipated. Whatever commission is applicable would then be forwarded to the RSO by the host with a note of explanation of charges. I much prefer having a third party manage all financial details. However, how you handle money is totally up to you and the RSO with whom you decide to work.

Independent Hosting

When handling reservations yourself, you will naturally need to create reservation and confirmation forms. The confirmation should be made out in duplicate for your records as well as for transfer to a simple calendar. This calendar will help eliminate the dreaded double-booking problem over which we all have an occasional nightmare. These various records will serve as accounting and IRS proof of business activity, as well as income accountability.

For these and any other forms and methods of record-keeping, you can get ideas from B&B inns and hotels and their brochures. Professional designers and printers are another source of help.

A letter of confirmation on your letterhead (with logo, line drawing of home, or other special identification) is perfectly appropriate, as long as all of the business matters are carefully spelled out. There is no one right way, only your way! Again, copies should be retained for your files, and to serve as proof of request, should problems arise at check-in time.

Along with the confirmation, I suggest you send a personal letter and map to your house, with directions from major freeways and airports. Just as the reservation form will draw a picture of your future guest, the confirmation enclosures will give the traveler a better profile of you. Now is the time to spell out house rules. They may be a part of the "Dear Guest" letter and/or detailed on the reservation confirmation.

- The Lavender Goose Room has a king-sized bed, dressing room, large sitting area: $50 private bath; $40 shared.

- Raggedy Ann Room has twin beds: $35/1; $40/2.

- Laura Ashley Blue Room has twin bed with private bath: $40.

- Room prices do not include applicable taxes.

- With a deposit of the first night's charge, your room will be held until arrival. Full refund will be issued if canceled one week prior to arrival, less a $10 handling fee.

Sample B&B Reservation Request Form (for Independent Hosts)

THE MATHEWS HOUSE
1111 Madrid Avenue
Los Angeles, CA 96543   (818) 000-0000

Name: _____

Address: _____

State: _____ ZIP:_____ Phone: (   ) _____

Occupation: _____ Work Phone: (   ) _____

Driver's License or Passport No.: _____

Number of Adults: _____Number & Ages of Children: ____

Arrival Date: _____Approximate Time: _____

Departure Date: _____Number of Nights: _____

Number of Rooms Needed: _____Will You Have/Rent a Car? _____

Bed Preference: Twins _____King/Queen _____

Bath Preference: Shared _____Private _____Don't Care _____

Do You Smoke? _____Any Allergies? _____

Special Requests: _____

Reference: _____

Address: _____

Phone: (   ) _____Relationship: _____

We cannot accommodate pets or children under age fourteen. In consideration of other guests, we ask that there be no smoking indoors. Check-in: After 3:00 P.M. Checkout: 12:00 noon. Luggage storage available.

Sample B&B Reservation Confirmation Form (for Independent Hosts)

THE MATHEWS HOUSE
1111 Madrid Avenue
Los Angeles, CA 96543   (818) 000-0000

GUESTS:

ACCOMMODATIONS (all include continental breakfast):

☐ Single bed   Lavender Goose Room   ☐
☐ Twin beds $50 private bath ☐
☐ King-sized bed $40 shared bath ☐
☐ Bath shared   Raggedy Ann Room   ☐
☐ Bath private $35/1; $40/2

Rate per night: _____ Laura Ashley Blue Room, $40 ☐
Number of nights: _____ Other Features   ☐
Total room fee: _____
Tax: _____
Other charges: _____ Arrival date: _____
Total Due: _____ Arrival time: _____
                             Departure date: _____

Balance due on arrival. Please pay with cash, money order, or traveler's check. First night prepaid guarantees room. Refund issued up to one week prior to scheduled arrival, less $10 handling fee. Check-in: After 3:00 P.M.   Checkout: 12:00 noon.

- Please indicate room preference, if any. (Lavender Goose and Raggedy Ann can be used as a suite with shared bath to accommodate four.)

- All rates include evening wine and extended continental breakfast.

- Swimming pool available May through September.

- The Mathews B&B is located within walking distance of free tennis, golf course, library, public transportation, and park. Five minutes from Universal Studios. Ten minutes from downtown L.A., Hollywood, Beverly Hills, and major Valley studios. Thirty minutes to LAX, ten minutes to Burbank Airport. Airport pickup can be arranged.

Checkout

Departure day is generally a hectic one and guests are usually anxious to get an early start. If this is the case, last-minute gestures will be rushed. We say most of our good-byes the night before while handling any money matters (charges for equipment rental, use of the phone, extra meals, etc., plus room charges if not handled upon arrival) that need to be finalized. The next morning we try to stay in the background as much as possible, but quickly check bedrooms before guests can get far down the street. Travelers seem to leave some little thing behind most of the time, so do take a fast look as they get settled into the car. It will save a lot of aggravation later.

Evaluation Request for Guest Comments

If you wish to leave a card or note requesting guest feedback on your B&B methods, make certain to take them in stride. You are opening yourself up for comparison to commercial B&B establishments, hotels, motels, every place the traveler has been. In addition, with the barrage of media hype and the glamorization of B&B, many first-time B&Bers may expect grander treatment than you provide, forgetting that yours is a far more reasonably priced situation than one they may have read about.

Sample Evaluation Form

Any comments that will help us enhance the hospitality and comfort of our guests would be appreciated:

_____

_____

If you would like us to mail our brochure to any of your friends, please list them here:

_____

I hope your stay with us was all you anticipated and more!

Leave-Taking

It's always nice to do a little something extra for guests when they leave, to let them know you enjoyed having them and appreciate their business.

- An Orlando, Florida, host takes photos of guests before they leave and adds them to her gallery of new friends in the hallway.

- Other hosts will take Polaroids for exchanging on the spot with the travelers.

- Most travelers carry a camera and want photos of you and your home. Offer to pay for copies or ask to borrow the negatives in a thank-you letter.

- Picnic boxes for a snack while on the road are a welcome optional extra you might suggest to guests.

- Otherwise, a tiny farewell packet of your favorite cookies (or an item particularly enjoyed and commented on by the departing guest) could be given free of charge.

Follow Up: Keep in Touch

Your relationship should not end when guests leave. Repeat business and recommendations are important and can be generated by staying in touch. Consider the following:

- A thank-you letter telling guests how much you enjoyed their visit.

- Holiday greeting cards.

- An occasional newsletter on B&B stationery. Update guests and those who have made an inquiry. Tell them about changes in the B&B, family activities, interesting visitors, new tourist attractions, anything that may encourage a return visit.

- Offer special return discounts to former guests.

- Offer next-visit discount of 10% of the entire bill for referring others (make certain friends mention the name for credit). A thank-you card/I.O.U. could go to the referring party.

- Create special offerings that might entice guests to return.

- Discounts to senior citizens (encourage guests to bring older relatives next time).

- Last day free on one-week bookings.

- Holiday promotions (Thanksgiving, Easter, New Year's Day, Halloween, St. Patrick's Day, Valentine's Day).

- Special events (see section on Sure Ways to Improve Business, Chapter 4).

- Package deals (check major newspaper travel sections on Sunday for ideas).

- Distribute copies of press articles on B&B in general and yours in particular. Attach a personal note or line.

In other words, keep the connection alive.

When Guests Become Friends

One day you may find that a guest who arrived a stranger has become a friend; this is one of the priceless bonuses that can come with hosting. Suddenly there is a friend to visit in faraway England if and when you travel across the Atlantic. Soon you may have invitations throughout the world—invitations you fully intend to accept one day.

We have had a few such situations. When one beautiful French family changed their itinerary to spend more time with us, they were no longer paying guests. How could we possibly charge people who wanted to take our daughter home for the school year in Pau? Naturally, they became as dear to us as our most beloved friends, and traveled halfway across Europe to visit me for an evening a few years later. Last summer one of my children spent several weeks with them in France, and another time at their vacation spot in Spain. They have never returned to the United States; however, we write on occasion and will meet again if time will allow, either here or there.

The loss of income from a change in relationship will be minimal; and profits enjoyed from this newfound friendship will be uncountable. I hope that B&B will bring a few such beautiful surprises to you, for the sharing of cultures face to face is a terribly special and unforgettable part of life. You will only understand the joy such unexpected friendships bring when it happens to you.

CHAPTER 8

Publicity and Promotion

If you are working with reservation services, a good deal of publicity will be generated directly by them, since B&B is currently the media's darling. RSO success depends on publicity and inquiries will, of course, be directed to member hosts.

Hosts may advertise in the numerous directories and work either independently or have contact made through an RSO. When the reservation service is listed as your contact number, privacy is protected, yet yours will be the home requested, since descriptions and pictures (if you pay for the inclusion of a photo or line drawing) will be of that one home—yours.

Independent hosts can maintain anonymity by using a post office box for mail contact and a telephone answering service or answering machine during "off" hours. If you plan carefully, you'll have no uninvited midnight arrivals or unsolicited calls.

Self-Promotion

Encourage the editor of your local paper's travel section to mention B&Bs, and yours in particular, as possible housing alternatives during special events or at any time when an unusual amount of tourist activity might create a crush on hotel space.

Don't neglect the English-language newspapers that are published throughout the world. If you speak other languages, contact the respective tourist boards, consulates, and newspapers.

How much better it is to stay in another country when there is someone with whom one is able to communicate.

If the media requests a host home for picture purposes, be available. Though the story may be of a very general nature, publicity never hurts. Readers of the article just may specify the B&B they want is yours. Being written about seems to add credibility to any business; B&Bs are no exception. Have a media kit ready for last-minute publicity requests.

Volunteer to speak at local organization meetings. Tell the rotary club, the garden club, or your church group about B&B—and yours.

Let local caterers and wedding consultants know about you. Out-of-town guests need reasonable accommodations.

Nearby universities and corporations are always looking for short-term lodging for visiting and/or newly transferred lecturers and employees. Relocation services would welcome knowledge of your business. In fact, you could develop your own personalized relocation service as an adjunct to the B&B.

What about hospitals and nursing homes? Again, visitors need a place to stay that is warm and inviting, particularly if the purpose of the visit is not the happiest of occasions. Preoperative testing can be done as an outpatient, with B&B cost much lower than inpatient room charges.

Take advantage of your other abilities and incorporate them into your B&B. A nurse might use hers as a halfway house for patients not quite ready to return home, or for those who will return to an empty house. Get in touch with the nearby plastic surgeons and hospitals. Tell them what you have to offer. Leave a brochure with each. Newly discharged patients could save considerable anxiety and expense, knowing there is an option beyond a nursing home or convalescent hospital.

Teachers are very busy with B&B travel. Why not use this teaching credential to specialize in crash courses in English? You could work with several nationalities at one time giving TESOL (English as a Second Language) classes.

Someone who signs might have a B&B for the hearing-impaired, together with special sightseeing tours and activities created for this group. A B&B with capability to handle the handicapped, particularly with wheelchair access to the home, could offer additional services, such as taking guests to theater, restaurants, and other tourist attractions that provide proper ramps.

There is no end to the special interest groups that can be helped in the warm, personalized, caring environment of B&B. See Specialized Referral Service Listings.

Promotional Materials

Unless their B&B is on commercially zoned property, Homestay hosts are usually forced to limit advertising to an occasional mention in industry newsletters, inclusion in directories, membership (and subsequent listing) in B&B associations, and reservation service mailings. Word-of-mouth referrals from friends and former guests become an important adjunct to the overall promotional quest. Take advantage of all of the above to improve visibility.

Whether you are working through an RSO or independently, a business card, stationery, and/or brochure that includes all the pertinent information about your B&B are absolutely necessary if you want to project a professional image.

Create a logo that can be used on all printed materials your potential and current guests will see. They will be portable advertising and souvenirs that might create interest and new business.

A line drawing of your house, or monograms, are quite inexpensive and effective. Both can be enlarged or reduced to suitable proportion for a myriad of uses. The colors of ink and paper you choose will help create a strong statement as well. Again, look at the materials used by large inns and hotels. They have paid small fortunes for consultants and advertising help. Since artwork and design can be expensive, if you lack the ability to do it yourself, contact local art schools or community colleges. Students need samples for their portfolios and letters of recommendation. They will be happy to work for a nominal fee, especially when given creative credit.

Copyright-free artwork is available, and a few companies offer mail-order stationery with logo when you send a photo of your house.

Sources for Copyright-Free Artwork

Request free copyright-free and pictorial catalogues from:

- Dover Publications, Inc., 31 E. Second Street, Mineola, NY 11501

- *Dynamic Graphics, Inc.* 6000 N. Forest Park Dr., P.O. Box 1901, Peoria, IL 61656-1901

Artist's Sketch Stationery, Business Cards & Memo Pads

- Request free catalog from: *The Business Book,* Miles Kimball Company, 1 West Eighth Avenue, Oshkosh, WI 54906.

If you decide to try designing yourself, press-on letters and paste-up art can be fun to work with.

Uses for Your Logo

If you have a logo or picture of your home created for use on your brochure, you'll find you can also use it on:

- Stationery and envelopes.
- Postcards.
- Reservation request form.
- Reservation confirmation form.
- Business cards.
- Paper coasters.
- Cocktail napkins.
- Paper guest towels.
- Design motif on craft items in rooms:
  - Pillows.
  - Quilts.
  - Wall hangings.
  - Bed linens.
  - Towels.
- B&B newsletter.
- Thank-you notes.
- Menus . . . for breakfast, tea service.
- T-shirts or other promotional items.
- Bathrobes.

- Tent cards on dressers.
- House rules.

In other words, wherever you place a printed word about your B&B, you should use your identifying mark.

Your Brochure

Your brochure can be used as a business card, a mailer in answer to queries, an attachment to publicity releases and letters to travel editors, and a "throwaway" to be left at travel agencies, automobile clubs, visitor and convention bureaus, and any other location prospective travelers might visit. One of my students traveled through Europe last year leaving a trail of brochures along the route. This deductible expense is already having results for her.

Since this is the only promotional material most potential guests will see, make certain that it expresses you and your lifestyle. Include all details of your home, along with main house rules.

I suggest the format be in two parts. The first section should be of expensive, heavy-stock paper, folded in two or three (to fit a number ten-size business envelope). Information on this folder should be basic and constant. Collect and review commercial inn mailers for ideas and see the following pages for specific wording "lifted" from sample brochures.

A separate "insert" sheet can be of matching color but of cheaper quality paper, and should contain information that might conceivably change. This information can be updated for very little cost, while the "outside" brochure remains intact. Planned carefully, your basic "outside" brochure need never be changed. Include:

☐ Name of your B&B if different from your own; otherwise, your name (suggestions follow).

☐ Address.

☐ Telephone number and hours to call.

☐ Logo or line drawing (if you have one) of your home.

☐ Description of home and common areas.

111

☐ Bedroom descriptions.

☐ Bath information for each room.

☐ Details of breakfast and other amenities included in price.

☐ Description of area along with tourist attractions.

☐ Directions to house with simple map.

☐ Languages spoken.

☐ Specific rules regarding pets, children, liquor, smoking. All policies that might deter guests.

☐ Guest services.

Among items that might change from time to time, and would therefore be included in the insert:

☐ Price of each room (Descriptions could be here along with special decorating details).

☐ Deposit requirements.

☐ Cancellation and refund policy.

☐ Optional extras (specify costs or indicate an extra fee is charged for these services).

☐ Check-in and checkout times.

☐ Hours breakfast, tea, and other free services are provided.

☐ Applicable tax information.

☐ Parking details.

☐ Manner of payment (cash, traveler's check, credit card).

☐ Courtesy percentage paid to travel agents.

☐ Rollaway or "extra person in room" charge.

☐ Times of year you operate, year-round or seasonal (specify dates when closed).

☐ Rates subject to change.

☐ Special group and weekly rates.

The insert should always have B&B name, address, and telephone number as well, since it may be separated from the main brochure.

If a brochure is not your style, or you wish to give a less sophisticated appearance, a simple letter on your B&B stationery can be preprinted to include all the necessary information. A reservation card and reply envelope can be enclosed, along with sample guest menu and map. Find the format that makes you most comfortable. One hostess, who began her thriving B&B when widowed at the age of seventy-six, uses a simple, colored four-by-six-inch card with the basic information. Obviously, she prefers to put her money into advertising, for her ads appear alongside those of large commercial inns in several slick magazines. The publicity generated by her entry into business as a very senior citizen has done more than any fancy promotional material could ever hope to accomplish.

Sample Brochure Headlines

Bed & Breakfast in the Heart of _____.
An elegant B&B in the Style of a European Inn.
A B&B Within the City.
Bed & Breakfast in the _____'s Residence.
The _____, Your Elegant Home in _____.
Quaint, Convenient, Affordable English Country Decor at an Urban Inn.
_____, a Bed & Breakfast Establishment
_____ Guest House. "A Welcome Change of Place"
Bed & Breakfast by the Sea (Bay, Lake, etc.)
The _____, a Short-Term Residential Center.
_____, a Victorian Bed & Breakfast.
The _____House.
The _____Guest House.
_____, Guest Rooms in a Private Home.
_____, a Romantic Getaway.
_____, Historic Home Built in _____.
_____'s Cottage.
_____, a Rural Inn.
_____, a Country Inn.

Ideas for Brochure (or for Use in Reservation Form When Working Independently):

- These rates do not include _____ percent tax.

- Rate schedule $_____ and up, includes a country breakfast.

- Rates with shared bath begin at $_____ a day; with private bath begin at $_____ a day.

- All rates, plus _____ percent bed tax, are payable in advance.

- Prices range from $_____ to $_____.

- Each additional person $_____.

- Except as noted, rooms are double occupancy. Please add $_____ each additional guest (breakfast included).

- 10 percent discount Sunday through Thursday.

- Special weekly rates available.

- Substantial discounts for stays of two weeks or more.

- Rates subject to change without notice.

- Room rates include continental breakfast and complimentary wine and cheese.

- All rates include breakfast and evening social hour.

- The rates quoted include breakfast and afternoon tea.

- Let us pamper you with breakfast in bed or a tray in the seclusion of your own special room.

- Complimentary breakfast and tea-time refreshment.

- A continental breakfast may be served in your room, the dining room or (weather permitting) in the garden.

- Daily breakfast variety.

- Breakfast is available from 8:30–10:00 A.M.

- Breakfast is served by choice either in guest rooms or downstairs in the _____.

- Normally we serve only breakfast, but for that special event, or if you notify us within a week of your visit, we will be happy to prepare a custom picnic basket or cater a meal for two in your room. Picnics start at $_____ and the dinners at $_____.

- Cocktail hour at 5:00 P.M., sherry and hors d'oeuvres.

- For weekends, there is a minimum stay Friday through Sunday.

- There is a two-night minimum stay.

- There is a two-night minimum for weekends and holidays.

- Reservation deposit required and 48-hour cancellation notice.

- A _____ day's deposit is required to hold reservations. With _____ hours' notice, refunds are gladly given.

- With a deposit of the first night's charges, your room will be held until your arrival. Refund will be issued if you cancel 48 hours prior to scheduled arrival, less a $10.00 handling fee.

- Reservation deposit required and _____ hour cancellation notice.

- A deposit of 50 percent must be sent seven days in advance of your visit.

- All refunds are subject to a $10.00 service charge.

- Rooms with private bath cannot be guaranteed.

- As in Victorian times, the facilities are shared, however, with the number of bathrooms at the _____ B&B, the sharing will be minimal.

- Terrycloth robes are provided for your bathing comfort.

- Silk kimonos for after bathing and lounging comfort.

- Airbeds or futon hide-a-beds available for extra guests.

- All rooms have queen-sized beds and private baths.

- Check-in: After 3:30 P.M. Checkout: 12:00 noon.

- Checkout time is flexible.

- Check-in time between 2:00 and 6:00 P.M. Please let us know if you will arrive later than 6:00 P.M.

- Checkout time 11:00 A.M. Luggage storage available.

115

- Sorry, we aren't equipped to handle children under twelve or pets.

- We cannot accommodate pets or children.

- We accommodate, but do not encourage, children, for we do not have the facilities to entertain young guests.

- As our pets look upon our home as their own, we cannot allow other pets or smoking.

- Cats in residence.

- Please observe our no-pet policy.

- In consideration of other guests, we ask that there be no smoking indoors.

- Antiques protected in a smoke-free environment.

- Read the daily newspaper as you relax in the clean air, for smoking is not permitted in our B&B.

- Smoking is permitted throughout the house.

- Light sleepers should request a room in the rear.

- We will do our utmost to accommodate guests having other requirements.

- We pay 10 percent commission to travel agents.

- Open all week year-round.

- Off-street parking is available.

- Filled with antiques, fresh flowers and candy.

- Barbecue facilities.

- Books, games and cards are available for your pleasure.

- A baby grand piano awaits anyone who wants to play.

- Bicycles, tennis rackets available.

- Foreign languages spoken.

- Airport, train, bus depot service.

- Arrangements for sightseeing/art tours.

- Handicapped accessible room.

- The _____ B&B is available for private and business

entertaining, weddings, receptions, club meetings, charitable functions and other special events.

• Laundry facilities available on premises.

Advertising

Please don't think that advertising is essential to B&Bing. If you are planning small-scale hosting, RSO participation may be all you wish or need. In that case, this section is only food for thought.

Naturally, B&B hosts want to keep advertising expenditures to a minimum. However, any business will have slack periods, and through well-placed ads, we try to stimulate reservations during these times. In many cases, a strong push for publicity will create a flow of guests. If economic, weather, or holiday reasons suggest that no amount of spending will change the reservation picture, the time and money can be better used at a later date. Some B&Bs have found paid advertising brought no results whatsoever. Others credit all of their success to inclusion in B&B publications and membership organizations, along with RSO support. Still others have found that a few selective magazines catering to the traveler have paid off for them.

I suggest you read several issues of major travel publications and magazines such as *Sunset, California,* and *New York* that cater to travel, along with newspaper travel sections (specifically, the Sunday editions). Watch for advertising and see how often it is repeated. Repeat ads indicate results. Nobody is going to continue paying for an ad that isn't pulling. An inexpensive way to do this research is to visit the library for a few months on a regular basis. You will learn in a short time what advertising tactics, if any, you should try.

Some advertising will be automatic with listed membership in the various B&B RSOs, associations, and specialized agencies. Consider:

• Listing your B&B in several of the B&B publications sold in major book stores (see Chapter 12, "Sources and Resources").

• Membership in national B&B associations, which means automatic inclusion in the directories that they make available to the media, by mail, and in some bookstores.

● Joining RSOs for all of the above reasons. RSOs also actively promote *your* B&B in order to create commissionable bookings.

● Teaming up with other independent hosts for joint advertising. Innkeeping associations are being formed in almost every county in California for this purpose, as well as to promote B&B and to set basic standards for commercial members. Shared advertising will enable you to participate in a larger, more visible ad at lower cost and for an ongoing period of time. Many professionals believe advertising can only work well when repeated often.

● Finding out if and when your Yellow Pages will take B&B listings. Just remember that once your address and phone are published, you create the possibility of unwanted calls and arrivals.

Networking

I believe that word-of-mouth is the best form of advertising, particularly in service businesses. No amount of paid advertising has an impact as strong as the praise of a friend or acquaintance.

Membership in social and professional organizations of all kinds will create a nucleus of newscasters who in turn can spread your word. In addition, membership organizations specifically designed to provide information for and help to B&B hosts exist and should be considered. Look into the opportunities offered by each. They are profit-making ventures, so costs may not necessarily fit into your current budget, but be aware of their existence. You should know where they are, in case one day you wish to join.

☐ **TOURIST HOUSE ASSOCIATION OF AMERICA** The least expensive of all associations, the Tourist House Association of America charges a $15.00 annual membership fee. Association members are listed in *Bed & Breakfast, U.S.A.*, a best-selling travel book available in every major bookstore in America, as well as by mail. Regional conventions and seminars are conducted, and the Association publishes a quarterly newsletter. Association members are not personally inspected, but travelers are requested to evaluate experiences at member homes in order to weed out any that do not meet the expected standards. "Cleanliness, Comfort, and Cordiality" is the Association motto. The inclusion of your RSO or B&B in this widely circulated book makes it an advertising bargain. Contact:

Tourist House Association of America
Betty R. Rundback, director
P.O. Box 355A, Greentown, PA 18426
Telephone: (717) 857-0856

☐ **THE AMERICAN BED & BREAKFAST ASSOCIATION** Host
members pay an annual membership fee of $30.00, entitling them to
listing in the Association's *Hostlist,* and inclusion in the AB&BA publication *A Treasury of Bed & Breakfast.* Members also receive sub-
scriptions to *Shoptalk* and *Bed & Breakfast Guest,* and two semi-an-
nual issues of *Hostlist.* RSO and guest memberships are available as
well. Contact:

The American Bed & Breakfast Association
P.O. Box 23294, Washington, DC 20026
Telephone: (703) 237-9777

☐ **THE BED & BREAKFAST SOCIETY** $25.00 annual membership
fee includes a quarterly publication, *Bed & Breakfast World Magazine,*
the *Bed and Breakfast World Directory,* and unlimited B&B reservation and referral service, with trip planning, networking between B&B
guests, host homes, inns, and related organizations. Contact:

Bed & Breakfast Society
Kenn Knopp, coordinator
330 West Main Street
Fredericksburg, TX 78624
Telephone: (512) 997-4712

☐ **THE NATIONAL BED & BREAKFAST ASSOCIATION** $50.00 an-
nual dues include a subscription to the Association's newsletter, free
B&B referrals, and a B&B guide at a member's reduced price, as well
as national advertisement. Contact:

The National Bed & Breakfast Association
Phyllis Featherstone, president
148 East Rocks Road, P.O. Box 332
Norwalk, CT 06852
Telephone: (203) 847-6196

Other organizations in the business community that may be of
interest and help to you include:

119

☐ **THE NATIONAL ALLIANCE OF HOMEBASED BUSINESS-WOMEN** P.O. Box 306, Midland Park, NJ 07432
Telephone: (201) 784-0229
A national, non-profit organization of about 2,000 women dedicated to promoting, supporting, and stimulating personal, professional, and economic growth among women who work from home. Chapters are forming throughout the United States, with national conventions held annually. Membership (national) $30.00. Contact for the chapter nearest you, or start your own!

☐ Chamber of commerce.

☐ Visitors and convention bureau.

☐ Colleges and university alumni associations.

☐ Singles groups.

☐ Fraternal organizations.

☐ Religious groups.

☐ Political commissions.

☐ Volunteer organizations of every kind. Personal as well as business satisfaction is enhanced.

☐ Hobby and sport clubs.

☐ Activist organizations.

☐ Organizations to which family members belong: PTA, Girl and Boy Scouts, spouse's business and social networks.

Most of these organizations have announcements and newsletters in which free or tax-deductible advertising and publicity may be placed.

These same groups have fund-raisers of all kinds. A gift certificate for a weekend at your B&B would make a wonderful door prize or auction donation (again tax-free, and full of promotion potential).

CHAPTER 9

B&B Host Profiles

B&B hosts come in every size, shape, and income category, and host for any number of reasons.

Jean and Bob

Jean and Bob, childless and semi-retired, use B&B primarily as a means to liven up what was becoming a boring lifestyle. Theirs is a small, simple, suburban Seattle home in a rather nondescript neighborhood. Neither the architecture nor decorating indicate any specialness, yet their home is occupied regularly. One reason for this activity is the location; Seattle is a thriving city, steadily growing. Another reason is aggressive promoting by the couple and their membership in several RSOs, as well as listings in numerous directories. Not the least of the reasons for this busy schedule is the fact that they intentionally keep room rates low, following a rather typically English B&B style, providing simple needs at low prices for undemanding guests. They prefer to be busy and, incidentally, to earn more by doing volume business.

Arthur and Joanne

On the other side of the spectrum is a prominent couple, Arthur and Joanne. They own a breathtaking home in a fashionable Los Angeles neighborhood. Travelers can anticipate paying handsomely to stay in this antique-filled, yet luxuriously cozy mansion. The hosts obviously don't want for money. Why should such a couple wish to risk the intrusion of strangers? Joanne loves people and finds the newness of each situation stimulating. But Arthur is a far more private person, and though he enjoys occasional hosting, often feels his privacy is invaded. At that point, his wife is wise enough to recognize the mood change and ceases B&B operations until they once again agree that guests will be welcomed by both. Since their personal friends range from film actors to day laborers, and interests are equally varied, is there any wonder B&B is fascinating for both these hosts and their fortunate guests? This couple is very mobile as well; they travel extensively and on whim. They have few guests, but when they do, a red carpet is laid out and the hosts cannot do enough. With such spacious surroundings, everyone has breathing room amidst luxury; it's not unlike staying at a fine inn at Homestay prices.

Bernice

Bernice, an elderly widow, enjoys B&B guests for companionship. Hers is a simple two-bedroom apartment on a busy city street, without any amenities. The RSOs that place travelers there try especially hard to match age and interests as well as room and rates; in Bernice's particular case, because she lives alone, her preference is to have single female travelers or older couples. Supplementing her Social Security is another motivating factor. When her late husband was in the military, they shared wonderful travel experiences, and Bernice's interest in faraway places has never waned. Though reduced to armchair travel due to severe arthritis, she manages to vicariously enjoy her visitors' stories and regales them with a few of her own. Naturally, due to fewer amenities, her fees must be lower than those charged by Joanne and Arthur.

Bernice is always home and available for guests, but her budget will not allow for much advertising and promotion. In addition, she wishes to keep a low profile for safety reasons. She also has limited space in her Philadelphia apartment, so she must weigh the positives and negatives carefully before deciding to have guests. As an apartment renter, Bernice has fewer tax writeoffs than a homemaker has to offset her income. Bernice must consider Social Security laws with regard to age and the income she is allowed to earn before she loses benefits. She must ascertain all of this from her nearest Social Security office. B&B may be profitable for her only up to a point.

Marie and Jim

Marie and Jim are a young couple with a growing family and a huge mortgage. Marie can no longer work full time due to home involvement, so she supplements the family income with several home-based businesses. Not only does this money come in handy at tax time, but it helps keep her in touch with the real world. As Marie says, she has actually been able to increase her creativity and self-confidence while producing income, and feels this new independence and identity are a direct result of the combination of B&B and her numerous craft outlets. She plans to add yet another home business when the babies are older, finding home-based business a welcome alternative to the part-time outside jobs that had been her only other option before. Marie uses the garage of their suburban Dallas home as a workshop, and has two spare bedrooms available for paying guests. She wonders about the future when the children will need separate rooms but, like Scarlett O'Hara, will worry about that tomorrow. In the meantime, the girls share a room, and B&B is giving more security to this expense-burdened young family. Marie sells much of her craft work to B&B guests, who enjoy taking home a tangible souvenir. She is thinking of enlarging this area of her business, but is proceeding slowly because there are just too few hours in her busy day.

It would seem that Marie and Jim have more net income than the others we have discussed, because of the additional possibility of sales of craft work to visitors. On the other hand, only one of their bedrooms will be available indefinitely; the second may have to be turned into a child's bedroom. In addition, families with young children may not have time to accommodate guests as often as they would like, even though a "homemaker" is present every day. The flip side of this coin, though, is that a home with young people present would be more appealing to travelers with small children, thereby opening up the possibility of extra income from babysitting and other child-related activity (see the section on extra ways to make money). Determination of potential net in this situation is difficult to assess.

The amount of earnings differs with each of these families for a variety of reasons. The homes have different numbers of available rooms at varying prices and with obviously different amenities. Occupancy is determined by season and location.

For these and other reasons (see Chapter 4, Money Matters), it is impossible to predict occupancy and, therefore, potential income. However, a simple analysis can be made of your individual home, and a potential profit and loss can be determined. Base this estimate on the number of rooms available multiplied by the number of days you intend to do business. Unlike the commercial innkeeper or hotel owner, you do not have a staff to manage a 365-day operation. However, neither do you have the payroll expenses that go along with a year-round business plan. You also have one of the most desirable of all possible worlds—business flexibility. Flexibility to open and close, as vacations, family obligations, and other interests attract you. You are not married to the business. It is a sideline avocation and should be thought of as extra income or one of several part-time businesses that may total full-time commitment.

Estimated Profit-and-Loss Statement

Total Estimated Income

1. _____ room at $_____ × _____days = $_____
2. _____ room at $_____ × _____days = $_____
3. _____ room at $_____ × _____days = $_____
4. _____ room at $_____ × _____days = $_____
5. Extra services provided × no. of guests $_____
6. Retail sales (crafts, gifts, etc.) $_____
   Total estimated annual gross income $_____

Estimated Expenses

1. Cost of services provided (5, above) $_____
2. Cost of sale items (6, above) $_____
3. Food (cost per person x no. guests) $_____
4. Utilities (% based on no. days x no. guests) $_____
5. Advertising & promotional expenses $_____
6. Insurance (proportionate use) $_____
7. Licenses $_____
8. Auto expenses (depreciation & mileage) $_____
9. Supplies (bath, cleaning, linens) $_____
10. Maintenance & repairs $_____
11. Office (Stationery, postage, brochures) $_____
12. Membership fees in B&B organizations $_____
13. Commissions to RSOs and travel agents $_____
14. Legal, accounting, bookkeeping expenses $_____
15. Other $_____
    Total estimated annual gross expenses $_____

$ Annual Gross Income
− Annual Gross Expenses

Total Estimated Gross Profit
− Taxes (state, federal, city)
− Depreciation

$ Estimated Net Profit

To estimate the potential B&B room gross profit, simply multiply the number of nights each room is available times the cost per room, and add.

Example:

2 bedrooms available weekends only

1 room w/private bath at $50 × 104 days	= $5200
1 room w/shared bath at $40 × 104 days	= $4160
Total potential income rented 100% Gross	$9360
Less Expenses	$____
Net	$____

Jean and Bob's estimate would look like this:
2 bedrooms available year-round, rented ⅓ of the year.
   1 room—double w/private bath at $40 × 120 days
                                          = $4800
   1 room—single w/shared bath at $25 × 120 days
                                          = $3000

Total potential gross income	$7800
Less estimated expenses	− 3900

To increase profit, estimated expenses might be refigured, cutting down costs wherever possible, though many will be fixed expenses (such as your mortgage) and unvarying.

Joanne and Arthur's three spare bedrooms, if available year-round for rental, could produce a sizable income if occupied full time. However, with their other interests they prefer an occasional guest, earning a relatively small net profit. Renting to one couple, just one time per month, a realistic net potential would be:

$50 per night/couple (3-night average) 1 × month =

$150 mo. × 12 mos.	= $1800.00
Less estimated expenses	500.00
Net estimated profit	1300.00

In this case, there are few estimated expenses, inasmuch as Joanne and Arthur belong to just one reservation service (paying only 20% commission), do no promoting on their own, have no formal brochure or mailing expenses, and consider the only other outlay to be the nominal cost of food and a small utilities expenditure. Since their homeowners' insurance covers two paying guests, theirs is an almost pure profit, requiring little bookkeeping.

Bernice wants to keep things simple, but would also like to earn as much money as Social Security rulings make feasible. Her net estimate looks as follows:

1 bedroom available year-round, rented ⅓ of the year.

1 bedroom/shared bath $35/couple (3-night average stay) × 120 days	= $4200.00
Less estimated expenses	1465.00
Net estimated profit	2735.00

In addition to the 20% average commission, Bernice considers other expenses to be approximately as follows:

Commission to reservation services at 20%	$840.00
Breakfast—120 days × 2 persons × $1.00 each	240.00
Supplies	15.00
Maintenance & repairs (apartment)	50.00
Membership fees in RSOs	35.00
Stationery & other office expenses	50.00
Promotional & advertising expenses	15.00
Taxes and licenses	120.00
Bookkeeping & accounting fees	100.00
Total estimated expenses	1465.00

Due to Marie's various small businesses, she must file separate schedules for each business, along with their regular tax form. Profits and losses combine to be included on the 1040 form, and in those years Marie has a profit, she must pay her own Social Security taxes, since she is essentially self-employed. However, she has the added advantage of being able to set aside the allowable IRA and Keogh savings, which offset earnings and create a sizeable nest egg when allowed to accumulate. This forced savings, tax-deductible, gives a measure of security to these young people. Their bills are so plentiful that Marie feels they would never be able to save otherwise and, as she says, when the money is in her pocket, it is too easy to spend on the darling toys and children's clothing that tempt her.

Each family looks at B&B from a different perspective. All know they will never get rich from the experience, at least not rich in the sense of monetary wealth. But each finds personal gains far exceeding the figures listed above.

Again, speak with a tax attorney, an accountant, and/or a knowledgeable SBA authority to fully learn the ramifications of profit-and-loss statements. Certain expenses will be fixed, others variable. The only thing guaranteed will be those fixed expenses and assets.

Naturally, as discussed in Chapter 4, Money Matters, if you are considering B&B as a hobby through which you'd like to meet new friends, a far less sophisticated outlook is necessary. Since hobby profit is taxable and expenses are deductible only to the extent of profit, a break-even point would be ideal; hobby hosting would make no profit to be taxed, nor would it cost anything either. Just be certain to retain every seemingly unimportant receipt relating to B&B for end-of-year appraisal.

CHAPTER 10

Common Complaints

Guest Complaints

Hosts cannot be at home when guests wish to check in.
Resolution: If possible, hosts, of course, should be at the door to welcome new arrivals. When absolutely impossible, a relative or close friend must be available. At the very least, hire an "inn-sitter," the way commercial inns do, for such an emergency. If this last resort is necessary, teach the sitter exactly how you behave with your guests. Act out a typical arrival, going through all of the pleasantries, necessities, and above all, the apologies for the absent host (a sideline business for a host/hostess would be to offer services to other B&Bs for just such an occasion). This substitute should stay in your home until your return—not because you fear for your worldly goods, but as a help to the traveler. I would be quite unhappy to arrive at an unattended home, and hope that these emergency measures are rarely, if ever, used. *Never* leave a key with the neighbor or under a doormat. That would be the height of rudeness.

Family pets unexpected by traveler.
Resolution: This situation should never occur, but does. Every RSO you work with should have knowledge of any animals in your household; all travelers should inquire before booking, should there be any reason for preferring a petless household. Unfortunately, even we had a difficult pet situation come up. A very late arrival neglected to tell us of her severe allergies. The resulting

asthma attack was quite frightening. We hastily said our good-byes the next morning and sent her to the nearest motel. Since that horrifying incident, we keep information on the nearest motels near the telephone bulletin board. Somewhere there had been a lack of communication; the RSO involved was aware of our menagerie. I believe our guest (a scientist herself, married to a doctor) simply forgot to mention her allergies. If you book independently, don't forget to warn guests about your pets. And if you allow guests to bring pets, whether you have one or not, be sure to inform all concerned parties—other guests, RSOs—since non-pet-owning guests might object.

Lack of private bath.
Resolution: This problem has been discussed elsewhere, but it is essential to mention it here. If your guests will have to share a bath, make absolutely sure that RSOs or your own reservation confirmation states that this is indeed the situation. Under no circumstances should one change a guest from private to shared bath in order to take another reservation. Turn down a booking, if necessary, but don't alter a reservation without notifying guests, unless to upgrade it without charge.

Inadvertently booking incorrect bed size.
Resolution: This has happened to us in commercial inns on occasion. When a double bed room was mistakenly set aside and the requested king was already occupied, we received apologies and a refund of the difference from the innkeeper, but the discomfort was still felt. I would like to think this was an innocent error, but I often wonder if the inn was simply trying to fill two rooms, and the last arrival (my husband and I) were the unfortunate ones. Again, reservations (particularly when guaranteed in advance, as ours were) should be delivered as promised. There can be a sincere mistake; nobody is perfect. However, if guest comfort is involved, the simple act of changing rates to the normal lower fee is inadequate; a personal gesture is called for—flowers, a box of candy, but something special!

Homeowners retire before guests return home.
Resolution: Inasmuch as guests are paying to use the facilities, homeowners cannot force their sleeping habits on others. If giving a house key is simply out of the question (and I truly cannot understand why this should be a problem, for the finest and most

luxurious inns give keys to guests), then one must simply wait up until everyone is home for the night. If loss of keys is the owner's concern, a $25.00 key deposit may be charged, refundable when the key is returned. However, though I am aware this policy exists, I am also aware that it offends many people.

Other complaints heard from guests through the RSO grapevine include those below. They are all quite easily avoided:

Dirty bathrooms. One must take special care to clean scrupulously before, during, and after guest stays.

Uncomfortable bed. This is easily recognized. Homeowners should spend a night in the rooms before renting to anyone. Discover whether the bed sags, the *reading light* is ample, *floors* are warm enough (put a throw rug near the bed; peg-and-groove wood floors may be a decorator's delight, but few decorators must have been barefoot on them).

No back rest. Most guests enjoy reading or watching television in bed. If back rests are not provided, use extra pillows if headboards aren't padded.

Squeaky doors. Please get out an oilcan, or whatever is necessary to provide a good night's sleep for your guests.

Constructive criticism is invaluable. There will always be malcontents, the never-satisfieds, but their criticism can always be weeded out. The fact that we seek out suggestions indicates our sincerity in the B&B program.

Host Complaints

The complaints I hear most often from hosts and reservation services regard the thoughtlessness of some travelers. Among the worst offenses are:

Last-minute no-shows.
Resolution: Many homeowners simply refuse to take reservations at the last minute, and insist on a minimum deposit of one night's lodging, non-refundable if canceled within a week of arrival (refund rules vary with each RSO and Homestay host). Others give a partial refund if cancellation is made within a reasonable time. Many RSOs refuse to take telephone requests at all unless from known travelers. Others will return long-distance calls by "collect" only. The time and energy spent securing accommodations and matching host to guest is considerable. To do

all of that work only to be informed that other arrangements have been made, generally without the courtesy of a call, has outraged many a B&B service. As Jean Brown, of Bed & Breakfast International, says, she carefully screens guests in various ways, one of which is by not taking last-minute reservations. Jean's law: "Guests who plan in advance make good guests." And I will add that guests who pay in advance arrive.

Guests who arrive before or after prearranged check-in.
Resolution: Check-in time should be clearly stated on brochures and confirmation forms. Guests should be made aware that yours is an organized business with rules, like any other member of the lodging industry. Guests should be asked to write if schedules have changed, phone if planes are going to be delayed, and in all cases, to be aware that if arrival is not at the stated time, hosts will not sit at home waiting, unless they have been contacted about the new developments. Naturally, there are going to be occasional emergencies that nature seems to arrange at the most inopportune times, for either guest or host. If guests arrive early, express your feelings politely. If they're late, don't rush to change your plans; they may never arrive!

Guests who dominate the kitchen.
Resolution: Allow only limited use of the kitchen and then only at the convenience of family members. Permit unlimited use of the icemaker/ice trays. If guests need a portion of the refrigerator (and you choose to oblige), one vegetable crisper should suffice. I never allow any cooking on my premises; why court trouble? I once slightly relaxed that ruling, and before long, I felt like a stranger in my own kitchen. Never again!

Guests who dominate the telephone.
Resolution: Though I have never had problems with the payment of telephone bills, guests have on occasion had "telephonitis"—often even ignoring the Call Waiting alarm. We firmly but kindly tell them that this is a business phone and that calls must be limited in length. Another option is to have two lines, letting guests make and receive personal calls on the line used by family. The second line is reserved for all business use and can have an answering machine attached twenty-four hours a day for reservation purposes.

Guests lingering endlessly in the shared bath.
Resolution: Provide as much service within the individual bedrooms as possible in order to alleviate congestion. Ideally, each
bedroom should have a sink. If such extras as curling irons and
hair dryers are offered, suggest that they be used in the room and
returned to the bath when finished. A subtle sign can be hung in
the bath as a reminder to slowpokes. And keep reading materials
in any other room!

*Travelers who request reservation information and are never
heard from again.*
Resolution: This is to be expected in any kind of business. Obviously, a request for information cannot be construed as a reservation request. Consider a reservation made only when money
has been received. Otherwise, rooms will sit empty. In the case of
a two-room B&B, if one guest fails to show up and hasn't paid in
advance, income lost for the night is fifty percent. We cannot sur-
vive on such statistics. The time and expense involved in answering each request for reservation information personally may be
put to better use with professional brochures that can be em-
ployed in a myriad of other ways, as well. A handwritten line on
the brochure would still give a feeling of individualized attention,
while presenting a businesslike attitude at the same time.

Unexpected arrivals at the door.
Resolution: If host addresses are listed widely in brochures and
directories, it is entirely conceivable that one day a hopeful visitor
will arrive without reservations. I would pleasantly explain that
this is a private home, that it is necessary to make all reservations
in advance, ask the party to wait outside for a moment while you
get a brochure or business card and reservation request form, and
ask that they get in touch with you through proper channels the
next time they are in town! You might also direct unannounced
visitors to the nearest hotel or motel. Keep other lodging information handy. Incidentally, were a stranger to arrive at my door, prepaid or not, who caused me to worry or experience a terribly
negative reaction, I would *absolutely* refuse entry. Nothing is
more important than personal safety. No reservation service can
be one hundred percent sure at all times. No B&B host has the
ability to read character in a letter or over a telephone. If there was
any doubt in my mind whatsoever, I would hastily close the door
behind me, tell the would-be guest we had a sudden family emer-

gency and must leave instantly to catch a plane. Directing him or her to the nearest motel, I would guiltlessly return inside and lock the door. I repeat, *there has never, ever been a reason for me to use this tactic, but I would feel within my rights, were it necessary.* Of course, the RSO involved would have to be notified, and would, I am sure, be in full agreement with this stand.

Generally, we have had few complaints with guests. All have been honest. Some have been neat, others messy. Some have been gregarious, others placid and shy. All have conducted themselves well and behaved as guests should, and a few arrived as strangers, leaving as very dear friends. I cannot speak for all hosts, but among my many B&B acquaintances, absolutely none have had to refuse a guest entry to their home.

CHAPTER 11

Reservation Service Organizations (RSOs): National, Specialized, and Local

National Reservation Services

The majority of RSOs cater to a specific part of a state. Others cover entire states and may even extend into neighboring ones. Very few try to tackle the enormous job of handling bookings throughout the United States, much less other countries. You should contact the few that do, however, since each host needs as many resources for guests as possible.

The list of RSOs changes constantly, and is growing every day. This is not an easy business, nor is it a big money-maker, so some RSOs will undoubtedly close or be sold by the time this edition is off the presses. The successful RSOs, on the other hand, will expand and add phone lines, move to larger quarters, incorporate, etc. For these reasons, I include a form at the back of the book for updating information. Feel free to mail it to me and I will do my utmost to let readers know of any changes that occur. I hope that you will also tell me of the B&B changes that are happening in your individual areas. In this way we will all be able to make use of current information and create a truly successful network.

In addition to contacting the national services listed below, you should, of course, contact the "specialty" RSOs (if they apply) and the regional and local offices in your area. Though identified here by state in which the office is located, many state RSOs handle homes in other nearby places as well, so thoroughly investigate the entire list.

Each RSO will have its own membership rulings and restrictions. Some will visit your home to inspect it for suitability, and to help you decide what rates to charge. Others send paid representatives to do this job. Still others will handle everything by mail, perhaps asking that you submit a photo of the house for their files.

As a B&B Homestay host, I most appreciate meeting company owners or representatives in person. It suggests to me that they will also screen guests carefully. Naturally, if an RSO office is in a distant place, the company will have to rely on feedback from visitors.

Start writing and calling reservation services right away. It takes several weeks (sometimes longer) for a response. Don't wait until the rooms are finished. Good screeners have imagination and can envision results. Your personality is throughout the home already, as is your housekeeping attitude. Describe future plans and how soon you anticipate completion. Cleanliness and friendliness are of prime consideration. Reasonable prices are of prime importance. A flair for decorating is just a bonus!

Indicate in your letters that you wish information regarding both host and guest participation in the organization. The more questions on the guest reservation form, the more thorough a background you will have on the strangers in your home. Enclose a self-addressed, stamped business envelope if you wish a quick reply.

As you contact each reservation service, you might want to note which you contacted and when, for your own records as well as for future tax proof. Keep records of *everything*.

At this time, the reservation services with NATIONAL COVERAGE include:

● *Bed & Breakfast Hospitality*
823 La Mirada Avenue
Leucadia, CA 92024
(619) 436-6850

• *Bed & Breakfast International*
151 Ardmore Road
Kensington, CA 94707
(415) 525-4569

• *Bed & Breakfast League*
3639 Van Ness Street, N.W.
Washington, DC 20008
(202) 363-7767

• *Bed & Breakfast Registry*
P.O. Box 80174
St. Paul, MN 55108
(612) 646-4238

• *Bed & Breakfast Service (BABS)*
P.O. Box 5025
Bellingham, WA 98227
(206) 733-8642

• *Home Suite Homes*
1470 Firebird Way
Sunnyvale, CA 93087
(408) 733-7215

• *Hospitality Plus*
P.O. Box 388
San Juan Capistrano, CA 92693
(714) 496-7050

• *InnServ*
310 Jefferson Street, P.O. Box 301
Eaton, IN 47338
(800) 222-3209 or (317) 396-3209

• *International Spareroom (The)*
P.O. Box 460
Helena, MT 59624
(406) 449-7231

Specialized Reservation Services and Directories

RSOs and directories catering to special interest groups with similar backgrounds or tastes are available. Hosts and travelers wishing to share a common interest might include these among the organizations to contact.

- **B&B Ski America**
P.O. Box 5246   (702) 831-6350
Incline Village, NV 89450
Skiers can find lodgings near major winter sports areas through this organization.

- **Bay Hosts (formerly Bed-by-the-Bay)**
1155 Bosworth Street   (415) 334-7262/383-7430
San Francisco, CA 04131
Primarily for gays. Hosts worldwide.

- **Commissioned Host & Toast**
P.O. Box 2177   (301) 863-6525
Springfield, VA 22152
Homes in Washington, D.C., open to active and retired military personnel.

- **Educators Inn**   (617) 334-6144
P.O. Box 603
Lynnfield, MA 01940
150 hosts in 30 states accept education-affiliated guests.

- **Educators' Vacation Alternatives**
317 Piedmont Road   (805) 687-2947
Santa Barbara, CA 93105
For active or retired educators, this service sells a combined home exchange and B&B directory. Guests book directly with the host. Properties are described, along with rates and addresses. Include a statement identifying your past or present educational employment when requesting information.

- **Homecomings**
P.O. Box 1545
New Milford, CT 06776
A directory started within the Unitarian Church community, but open to "anyone who considers himself or herself a humanist." $8.95

covers registration as a Homecomings Traveler, a travel directory, and a personal travel-ID card. First time hosts pay a $10 fee to cover the costs of printing the listing.

● **League of Women Voters**
Members act as host in many metropolitan areas; call your local chapter for more information.

● **University Bed & Breakfast of Boston**
12 Churchill Street   (617) 738-1424
Brookline, MA
Serves professors, spouses, and companions visiting Boston for academic reasons.

● **American Historic Homes Bed & Breakfast**
P.O. Box 336   (714) 496-7050
Dana Point, CA 92629
Bed & Breakfast in private homes of historic significance throughout the United States.

● **Christian Bed & Breakfast**
P.O. Box 388   (714) 496-7050
San Juan Capistrano, CA 92693
A network of homes serving the Christian community.

● **Christian Hospitality**   (617) 947-2356 or 947-1230
P.O. Box Drawer D
Middleboro, Massachusetts 02346
Primarily in New England, but also other states, Canada, and overseas.

● **The Evergreen Club**
A concept developed by The American Bed & Breakfast Association, this membership club is open to people over 50. $35.00 annual membership includes a directory and a newsletter. B&B rates of $15.00 nightly per couple can be arranged directly between members. For details, write the American Bed & Breakfast Association. Attention: The Evergreen Club, P.O. Box 23294, Washington, DC 20026.

State & Regional Bed & Breakfast Reservation Services

ALABAMA

● *Bed & Breakfast Birmingham*　　　　　　　(205) 591-6406
P.O. Box 31328
Birmingham, AL 35222

● *Bed & Breakfast Mobile*　　　　　　　　　(205) 473-2939
P.O. Box 66261
Mobile, AL 36606

● *Bed & Breakfast Montgomery*　　　　　　　(205) 285-5421
P.O. Box 886
Millbrook, AL 36054

● *Brunton's Bed & Breakfast Agency*　　　　　(205) 259-1298
P.O. Box 1066
Scottsboro, AL 35768

ALASKA

● *Alaska Private Lodgings*　　　　　　　　　(907) 345-2222
P.O. Box 10135
Anchorage, AK 99511

● *Bed & Breakfast Southeastern Alaska*　　　　(907) 586-2959
526 Seward Street, Suite 102
Juneau, AK 99801

● *Dawson's Bed & Breakfast*　　　　　　　　(907) 586-9708
1941 Glacier Highway
Juneau, AK 99801

● *Fairbanks Bed & Breakfast*　　　　　　　　(907) 452-4967
P.O. Box 74573
Fairbanks, AK 99707

● *Ketchikan Bed & Breakfast*　　　　　　　　(907) 225-6044
P.O. Box 7814
Ketchikan, AK 99901

● *Stay With a Friend Bed & Breakfast*　　　　(907) 274-6445
3605 Arctic Boulevard, P.O. Box 173
Anchorage, AK 99503

ARIZONA

- ***Barbara's Bed & Breakfast***   (602) 886-5847
P.O. Box 13603
Tucson, AZ 85732

- ***Bed & Breakfast in Arizona***   (602) 995-2831
8433 N. Black Canyon Highway No. 160
Phoenix, AZ 85021

- ***Bed & Breakfast—Scottsdale***   (602) 998-7044
P.O. Box 624
Scottsdale, AZ 85252

- ***Mi Casa—Su Casa Bed & Breakfast***   (602) 990-0682
P.O. Box 950
Tempe, AZ 85281
B&Bs in Arizona, California, and Utah.

CALIFORNIA

- ***Bed & Breakfast Approved Hosts***   (805) 647-0651
10890 Galvin
Ventura, CA 93004

- ***Bed & Breakfast California Sunshine***   (818) 992-1984
22704 Ventura Boulevard #1984   (213) 274-4494
Woodland Hills, CA 91364-1394

- ***Bed & Breakfast Exchange***   (707) 963-7756
P.O. Box 88
St. Helena, CA 94574

- ***Bed & Breakfast Homestay***   (805) 927-4613
P.O. Box 326
Cambria, CA 93428

- ***Bed & Breakfast Hospitality***   (619) 436-6850
823 La Mirada Avenue
Leucadia, CA 92024
Host homes in California and around the globe.

- ***Bed & Breakfast in the Desert***   (619) 320-1676
104 S. Indian Avenue
Palm Springs, CA 92262

141

● **Bed & Breakfast International**   (415) 525-4569
151 Ardmore Road   (415) 527-8836
Kensington, CA 94707
B&B throughout the United States and Hawaii.

● **Bed & Breakfast of Los Angeles**   (818) 889-8870
32074 Waterside Lane   (818 889-7325
Westlake Village, CA 91361

● **Bed & Breakfast Reservations of Napa Valley** (707) 224-4667
1834 First Street
Napa, CA 94559

● **Bed & Breakfast of San Francisco**   (415) 931-3083
P.O. Box 349
San Francisco, CA 94101-0349

● **Bed & Breakfast of Southern California**   (714) 879-2568
P.O. Box 218
Fullerton, CA 92632

● **California Houseguests International**   (818) 344-7878
6051 Lindley Avenue, No. 6
Tarzana, CA 91356
B&B throughout California, the United States, and Europe

● **Carolyn's Bed & Breakfast Homes in San Diego** (619) 435-5009
P.O. Box 84776
San Diego, CA 92138

● **Co-Host, America's Bed & Breakfast**   (213) 699-8427
P.O. Box 9302
Whittier, CA 90608

● **Digs West**   (714) 739-1669
8191 Crowley Circle
Buena Park, CA 90621

● **El Camino Real Bed & Breakfast**   (818) 363-6753
P.O. Box 2906
Northridge, CA 91323-2906

● **Eyeopeners**   (213) 684-4428
P.O. Box 694
Altadena, CA 91001

● *Home Suite Homes*   (408) 733-7215
1470 Firebird Way
Sunnyvale, CA 93087
Most homes in Northern California, but they also book nationwide.

● *Hospitality Plus*   (714) 496-7050
P.O. Box 388
San Juan Capistrano, CA 92693
Homes nationwide.

● *Houseguests U.S.A., Inc.*   (714) 891-3736
14340 Bolsa Chica Road, Suite A
Westminster, CA 92683

● *Megan's Friends*   (805) 544-4406
1768 Royal Way
San Luis Obispo, CA 93401

● *Mona's B&B Homes*   (714) 676-4729
P.O. Box 1805 Rancho California
Temecula, CA 92390

● *Rent-A-Room International*   (714) 638-1406
11531 Varna Street
Garden Grove, CA 92640

● *Room Service-Inn Reservations*   (415) 543-4522
330 Townsend Street, No. 113   (800) 828-3567 in California
San Francisco, CA 94107   (800) 325-6343 outside California

● *San Diego Bed & Breakfast*   (619) 560-7322
P.O. Box 22948
San Diego, CA 92122

● *Seaview Reservations*   (714) 494-8878
P.O. Box 1355
Laguna Beach, CA 92652

● *Travelers Bed & Breakfast*   (714) 591-4647
P.O. Box 1368
Chino, CA 91710

● *Unique Housing*   (415) 658-3494
81 Plaza Drive   (415) 548-4430
Berkeley, CA 94705

● *University Bed & Breakfast*   (415) 661-8940
66 Clarendon Avenue   (415) 753-3574
San Francisco, CA 94114

● *Visitors' Advisory Service*   (415) 521-9366
1516 Oak Street #327
Alameda, CA 94501

● *Wine Country Bed & Breakfast*   (707) 539-1183
P.O. Box 3211   (707) 578-1551
Santa Rosa, CA 95403

COLORADO

● *Bed & Breakfast of Boulder*   (303) 442-6664
P.O. Box 6061
Boulder, CO 80306

● *Bed & Breakfast Colorado*   (303) 833-3340
P.O. Box 20596
Denver, CO 80220

● *Bed & Breakfast Rocky Mountains*   (303) 630-3433
P.O. Box 804
Colorado Springs, CO 80901
B&Bs in Colorado, Montana, New Mexico, and Wyoming.

● *Bed & Breakfast Vail Valley*   (303) 476-1225
P.O. Box 491
Vail, CO 81658

CONNECTICUT

● *Bed & Breakfast Ltd.*   (203) 469-3260
P.O. Box 216
New Haven, CT 06513

● *Covered Bridge Bed & Breakfast*   (203) 672-6052
West Cornwall, CT 06796
Homes in Connecticut, Massachusetts, and New York.

● *Nautilus Bed & Breakfast*   (203) 448-1538
133 Phoenix Drive
Groton, CT 06340
Connecticut and Rhode Island.

● *Nutmeg Bed & Breakfast*   (203) 236-6698
222 Girard Avenue
Hartford, CT 06105
Covers the entire state of Connecticut.

● *Seacoast Landings*   (203) 442-1940
21 Fuller Street
New London, CT 06320
Covers southeastern Connecticut.

DISTRICT OF COLUMBIA

● *Bed & Breakfast League Ltd.*   (202) 363-7767
3639 Van Ness Street, NW
Washington, DC 20008
Homes throughout the United States and abroad.

● *Bed 'n' Breakfast Ltd. of Washington, D.C.*   (202) 328-3510
P.O. Box 12011
Washington, DC 20005
Covers Washington, D.C., and outlying cities.

● *Sweet Dreams & Toast, Inc.*   (202) 483-9191
P.O. Box 4835-0035
Washington, DC 20008
B&Bs in Maryland, Virginia, and Washington, D.C.

DELAWARE

● *Bed & Breakfast of Delaware*   (302) 475-0340
1804 Breen Lane
Wilmington, DE 19810
Southern beach area, northern Delaware, and Pennsylvania.

FLORIDA

● *AAA Bed & Breakfast, Inc.*   (305) 628-3233
P.O. Box 1316
Winter Park, FL 32790

● *B&B Accommodations of Orlando*   (305) 352-9157
8205 Banyan Boulevard
Orlando, FL 32819

● *B&B of Southwest Florida*
P.O. Box 1032
Bradenton, FL 33506

● **B&B Suncoast Accommodations**   (813) 360-1753
8690 Gulf Boulevard
St. Petersburg Beach, FL 33706

● **Bed & Breakfast Central Gulf Coast**   (904) 438-7968
P.O. Box 12561
Pensacola, FL 32573

● **Bed & Breakfast Company**   (305) 661-3270
P.O. Box 262
South Miami, FL 33243

● **Bed & Breakfast Inc. of the Florida Keys** (305) 743-4118
5 Man-O-War Drive
Marathon, FL 33050

● **Florida & England Bed & Breakfast Accommodations** (813) 784-5118
P.O. Box 12
Palm Harbor, FL 33563
St. Petersburg, Tampa, Sarasota, Gulf Coast, and England.

● **Sarasota Bed & Breakfast**   (813) 365-1755
3230 S. Tamiami Trail
Sarasota, FL 33579

● **Tallahassee Bed & Breakfast Inc.**   (904) 421-5220
3023 Windy Hill Lane
Tallahassee, FL 32308

● **Tropical Isles B&B Co.**   (305) 361-2937
P.O. Box 490382
Key Biscayne, FL 33149

GEORGIA

● **At Home in Athens**   (404) 543-7928
120 Cedar Circle
Athens, GA 30605

● **Atlanta Home Hospitality**   (404) 493-1930
2472 Lauderdale Drive NE
Atlanta, GA 30345

● **Bed & Breakfast Atlanta**   (404) 875-0525
1801 Piedmont Avenue NE
Atlanta, GA 30324

● *Bed & Breakfast-Savannah*   (912) 238-0518
117 W. Gordon Street
Savannah, GA 31401

● *Hideaway Bed & Breakfast*   (404) 632-3669
Dial Star Route P.O. Box 76
Blue Ridge, GA 30513
Homes in Georgia, North Carolina, and Tennessee.

● *Home Hospitality*
1111 Clairmont Road Suite D4
Decatur, GA 30030

● *Intimate Inns of Savannah*   (912) 233-6809
19 W. Perry Street
Savannah, GA 31401

● *Quail Country Bed & Breakfast Ltd.*   (912) 226-7218
1104 Old Monticello Road
Thomasville, GA 31792

● *Savannah Historic Inns*   (912) 233-7666
1900 Lincoln Street
Savannah, GA 31401

HAWAII

● *Bed & Breakfast Hawaii*   (808) 822-1582
P.O. Box 449
Kapaa, HI 96746

● *Go Native, Hawaii, Ltd.*   (808) 961-2080
130 Puhili St.
Hilo, HI 96720
      or
P.O. Box 13115   (517) 349-9598
Lansing, MI 48901

● *Pacific Hawaii Bed & Breakfast*   (808) 262-6026
19 Kai Nani Place
Kailua, Oahu 96734 HI

ILLINOIS

● *Bed & Breakfast/Chicago, Inc.*   (312) 951-0085
1704 N. Crilly Court
Chicago, IL 60614
Chicago, suburbs, Indiana, Michigan, and Wisconsin.

INDIANA

● *InnServ*   (800) 222-3209
P.O. Box 301   (317) 396-3209
Eaton, IN 47338
Nationwide reservation service for B&B Inns and Homestays.

IOWA

● *Bed & Breakfast in Iowa, Ltd.*   (515) 277-9018
7104 Franklin Avenue
Des Moines, IA 50322

● *Bed & Breakfast of the Quad Cities*   (319) 359-4156
P.O. Box 488
Davenport, IA 52805

KANSAS

● *Kansas City Bed & Breakfast*   (913) 268-4214
P.O. Box 14781
Lenexa, KS 66215
Serves Missouri and Kansas, particularly, Kansas City and suburbs.

KENTUCKY

● *Bed & Breakfast in the Bluegrass*   (606) 873-3208
Rt. 1, P.O. Box 263
Versailles, KY 40383
Homes in Central Kentucky.

● *Kentucky Homes Bed & Breakfast*   (502) 635-7341
1431 St. James Court   (502) 452-6629
Louisville, KY 40208

LOUISIANA

● *Bed, Bath & Breakfast*   (504) 897-3867
P.O. Box 52466   (504) 891-4862
New Orleans, LA 70152

● *Bed & Breakfast, Inc.*   (504) 525-4640
1236 Decatur Street
New Orleans, LA 70116

● *Louisiana Hospitality Services*　　　　　(504) 769-0366
P.O. Box 80717
Baton Rouge, LA 70898
Hosts in Alabama, Arkansas, Louisiana, and Mississippi.

● *New Orleans Bed & Breakfast*　　　　　(504) 949-6705
P.O. Box 8163　　　　　　　　　　　　　(504) 949-4570
New Orleans, LA 70182
Bookings throughout the state and on the Gulf Coast.

● *Southern Comfort Bed & Breakfast Reservation Service*
2856 Hundred Oaks　　　　　　　　　　(504) 346-1928
Baton Rouge, LA 70808
Books Louisiana, Mississippi, New Mexico, New Zealand, and Tahiti.

MAINE

● *Bed & Breakfast Accommodations*　　　　(207) 594-8275
P.O. Box 805
Rockland, ME 04841

● *Bed & Breakfast Down East, Ltd.*　　　　(207) 565-3517
P.O. Box 547
Eastbrook, ME 04634

● *Bed & Breakfast of Maine*　　　　　　　(207) 781-4528
32 Colonial Village
Falmouth, ME 04105

MARYLAND

● *Amanda's Bed & Breakfast, Ltd.*　　　　(301) 821-8290
P.O. Box 42　　　　　　　　　　　　　　(301) 665-1333
Long Green, MD 21092
Baltimore, Eastern Shore, Annapolis, and other states.

● *The Traveller in Maryland*　　　　　　　(301) 269-6232
33 West Street　　　　　　　　　　　　(301) 261-2233
Annapolis, MD 21401
Also handles Delaware, Virginia, West Virginia, and England.

MASSACHUSETTS

● *Be Our Guest Bed & Breakfast*　　　(617) 641-3900 (in state)
P.O. Box 1333　　　　　　　　　　　　(617) 545-6680
Plymouth, MA 02360

● *Bed & Breakfast Areawide Cambridge & Greater Boston by Riva Poor*
73 Kirkland Street   (617) 576-1492
Cambridge, MA 02138
Also Cape Cod and the Islands.

● *Bed & Breakfast Associates—Bay Colony, Ltd.*   (617) 449-5302
P.O. Box 166 Babson Park Branch
Boston, MA 02157
Maine, New Hampshire, Vermont, Connecticut, and Eastern Massachusetts.

● *Bed & Breakfast Brookline/Boston*   (617) 277-2292
P.O. Box 732
Brookline, MA 02146
B&B in Boston, Cambridge, Brookline, Nantucket, and Cape Cod.

● *Bed & Breakfast Cape Cod*   (617) 775-2772
P.O. Box 341
West Hyannisport, MA 02672

● *Bed & Breakfast in Minuteman Country*   (617) 861-7063
8 Linmoor Terrace
Lexington, MA 02173
All homes within driving distance of Boston.

● *Berkshire Bed & Breakfast of Western Massachusetts*   (413) 783-5111
141 Newton Road
Springfield, MA 01118
B&Bs throughout central and western Massachusetts.

● *Christian Hospitality Bed & Breakfast*   (617) 947-2356
P.O. Box, Drawer "D"
Middleboro, MA 02346
Homes primarily in New England; some in Canada, overseas, and in other states.

● *Great Boston Hospitality*   (617) 734-0807
P.O. Box 1142
Brookline, MA 02146

● *Hampshire Hills B&B*   (413) 634-5529
P.O. Box 307
Williamsburg, MA 01096

● *Host Homes of Boston*   (617) 244-1308
P.O. Box 117
Newton, MA 02168

● *House Guests Cape Cod*   (617) 398-0787
P.O. Box 8
Dennis, MA 02638

● *New England Bed & Breakfast*   (617) 498-9819
1045 Centre Street
Newton, MA 02159
Primarily Boston; also "special" places throughout New England.

● *Orleans Bed & Breakfast Associates*   (617) 255-3824
P.O. Box 1312
Orleans, MA 02653
Covers entire Cape Cod region.

● *Pineapple Hospitality*   (617) 990-1696
384 Rodney French Boulevard
New Bedford, MA 02744
*Listings in Southeastern Massachusetts and Cape Cod. Covers
Maine, Massachusetts, New Hampshire, Rhode Island, Vermont, a
home in Bermuda, and one in Spain.*

● *Yankee Bed & Breakfast of New England*   (617) 749-5007
8 Brewster Road
Hingham, MA 02043
Covers South Shore and Boston areas.

MICHIGAN

● *B&B of Grand Rapids*   (616) 451-4849
344 College S.E.
Grand Rapids, MI 49503

● *Betsy Ross Bed & Breakfast*   (313) 647-1158
3057 Betsy Ross Drive
Bloomfield Hills, MI 48013
Statewide coverage.

● *Capital Bed & Breakfast*   (517) 468-3434
5150 Corey Road
Williamston, MI 48895
Lansing area.

● *Frankenmuth Area B&B*   (517) 652-8897
337 Trinklein
Frankenmuth, MI 48734

MINNESOTA

● *Bed & Breakfast Registry*　　　　　　　(612) 646-4238
P.O. Box 80174
St. Paul, MN 55108
A national network of homes.

● *Uptown Lake District Bed & Breakfast League*　(612) 872-7884
2301 Bryant Avenue　　　　　　　　　　　(612) 377-7032
Minneapolis, MN 55405

MISSISSIPPI

● *Lincoln Ltd. Bed & Breakfast*　　　　　(601) 482-5483
P.O. Box 3479
Meridian, MS 39301
Homes throughout the state, Memphis, New Orleans, and other states.

● *Natchez Pilgrimage Tours*　　　　　　(601) 446-6631
P.O. Box 347
Natchez, MS 39120

MISSOURI

● *Bed & Breakfast St. Louis*　　　　　　(314) 533-9299
4418 W. Pine
St. Louis, MO 63108

● *Lexington Bed & Breakfast*　　　　　　(816) 259-4163
115 N. Eighteenth Street
Lexington, MO 64067

● *Midwest Host Bed & Breakfast*　　　　(417) 782-9112
P.O. Box 27
Saginaw, MO 64864
Lists homes in Indiana, Illinois, Iowa, Missouri, Oklahoma, Texas, Arkansas, Minnesota, and New York.

● *Ozark Mountain Country Bed & Breakfast*　(417) 334-4720
P.O. Box 295
Branson, MO 65616
Homes in the Arkansas and Missouri Ozarks.

● *River Country Bed & Breakfast*　　　　(314) 965-4328
#1 Grandview Heights
St. Louis, MO 63131

● *Truman Country Bed & Breakfast*   (816) 254-6657
P.O. Box 14
Independence, MO 64050

MONTANA   (406) 257-4476

● *Western Bed & Breakfast Hosts*
P.O. Box 322
Kalispell, MT 59901
Covers area between Calgary, Alberta, Canada in the North, and Yellowstone National Park in the South.

NEBRASKA

● *Bed & Breakfast of Nebraska*   (402) 564-7591
1464 Twenty-eighth Avenue
Columbus, NB 68601

NEW HAMPSHIRE

● *New Hampshire Bed & Breakfast* (603) 279-8348
RFD 3, P.O. Box 53
Laconia, NH 03246

NEW JERSEY

● *Bed & Breakfast of New Jersey* (201) 444-7409
103 Godwin Avenue
Midland Park, NJ 07432

NEW MEXICO

● *Bed & Breakfast of Santa Fe*   (505) 982-3332
218 E. Buena Vista Street
Santa Fe, NM 87501

● *Accommodations Unlimited*   (505) 247-8834
2301 Yale Blvd. S.E., Suite A-2
Albuquerque, NM 87106

NEW YORK

● *A Reasonable Alternative*   (516) 928-4034
117 Spring Street
Port Jefferson, NY 11777
Most homes in Nassau & Suffolk counties.

● **Alternate Lodgings, Inc.**   (516) 324-9449
P.O. Box 1782
East Hampton, L.I., NY 11937
Covers the Hamptons from Westhampton to Montauk.

● **B&B Group (New Yorkers at Home) Inc.**   (212) 838-7015
301 E. Sixtieth Street
New York, NY 10022
Manhattan, Hampton Beaches, Long Island, and Acapulco, Mexico.

● **Bed & Breakfast Rochester**   (716) 223-8877
P.O. Box 444   (716) 223-8510
Fairport, NY 14450

● **Bed & Breakfast U.S.A., Ltd.**   (914) 271-6228
P.O. Box 606
Croton-on-Hudson, NY 10520
New York City, Hudson Valley, Connecticut, Saratoga, and Central New York.

● **Cherry Valley Ventures**   (315) 677-9723
6119 Cherry Valley Turnpike
Lafayette, NY 13084
Hosts throughout the state.

● **Hampton Bed & Breakfast Registry**   (516) 878-8197
P.O. Box 378
East Moriches, NY 11940
Homes throughout Long Island.

● **New World Bed & Breakfast**   (212) 675-5600
150 Fifth Avenue, No. 711
New York, NY 10011

● **North Country Bed & Breakfast Reservation Service** (518) 523-3739
P.O. Box 286
Lake Placid, NY 12946
Homes throughout Adirondacks, New York, and Vermont.

● **Rainbow Hospitality Bed & Breakfast**   (716) 283-1400
9348 Hennepin Avenue
Niagara Falls, NY 14304
B&B in Buffalo, Niagara Falls, and Rochester areas.

● **Urban Ventures, Inc. (Bed & Breakfast in the Big Apple)**
P.O. Box 426   (212) 594-5650
New York, NY 10024

NORTH CAROLINA

- *Bed & Breakfast of Asheville* (704) 258-9537
217-A Merrimon Avenue
Asheville, NC 28801

- *Bed & Breakfast in the Albemarle* (919) 792-4584
P.O. Box 248
Everetts, NC 27825
Northeastern area homes.

- *Charlotte Bed & Breakfast* (704) 366-0979
1700-2 Delane Avenue
Charlotte, NC 28211

OHIO

- *Buckeye Bed & Breakfast* (614) 548-4555
P.O. Box 130
Powell, OH 43065

- *Chillicothe Bed & Breakfast* (614) 772-6848
202 S. Paint Street
Chillicothe, OH 45601

- *Columbus Bed & Breakfast* (614) 444-8888
763 S. Third Street
Columbus, OH 43206

- *Private Lodgings, Inc.* (216) 321-3213
P.O. Box 18590
Cleveland, OH 44118
Most homes in metropolitan Cleveland area.

OKLAHOMA

- *Bed & Breakfast Oklahoma Style* (405) 946-2894
P.O. Box 32045
Oklahoma City, OK 73123

OREGON

- *Bed & Breakfast Oregon* (503) 245-0642
5733 S.W. Dickinson Street
Portland, OR 97219
Also handles homes on the islands of Hawaii, Oahu, Maui, Molokai; a few in California and Washington.

155

● *Bend Bed & Breakfast* (503) 388-3007
19838 Ponderosa Drive
Bend, OR 97702
B&Bs in Central Oregon.

● *Galluci Host, Hostels, B&B* (503) 636-6933
P.O. Box 1303
Lake Oswego, OR 97034

● *Griswold's Bed & Breakfast* (503) 683-6294
552 W. Broadway
Eugene, OR 97401

● *Northwest Bed & Breakfast, Inc.* (503) 246-8366
7707 S.W. Locust Street
Portland, OR 97223
*Homes in California, British Columbia, Idaho, Montana, Oregon,
Washington, Wyoming, Hawaii, and other states.*

PENNSYLVANIA

● *Bed & Breakfast Center City* (215) 735-1137/0881
1908 Spruce Street
Philadelphia, PA 19103

● *Bed & Breakfast in the Lancaster, Harrisburg, & Hershey Areas*
463 N. Market Street (717) 367-9408
Elizabethtown, PA 17022

● *Bed & Breakfast of Chester County* (215) 444-1367
P.O. Box 825
Kennett Square, PA 19348

● *Bed & Breakfast of Philadelphia* (215) 688-1633
P.O. Box 680
Devon, PA 19333-0680
B&B also in suburbs, Wilmington, Delaware, and New Jersey.

● *Bed & Breakfast of Southeast Pennsylvania* (215) 845-3526
P.O. Box 278, R.D. 1
Barto, PA 19504

● *Bed & Breakfast Pocono Northeast* (717) 472-3145
P.O. Box 115
Bear Creek, PA 18602

● **Pittsburgh Bed & Breakfast**   (412) 367-8080
2190 Ben Franklin Drive
Pittsburgh, PA 15237

● **Rest & Repast Bed & Breakfast Service**   (814) 238-1484
P.O. Box 126
Pine Grove Mills, PA 16868
Center regions of Pennsylvania.

RHODE ISLAND

● **At Home in New England**   (401) 294-3808
P.O. Box 25
Saunderstown, RI 02874

● **Bed & Breakfast Registry—Castle Keep**   (401) 846-0362
44 Everett
Newport, RI 02840

● **B&B of Rhode Island**   (401) 246-0142
P.O. Box 312
Barrington, RI 02806

SOUTH CAROLINA

● **Bay Street Accommodations**   (803) 524-7720
601 Bay Street
Beaufort, SC 29902

● **Charleston Society B&B**   (803) 723-4948
84 Murray Boulevard
Charleston, SC 29401

● **Low Country Bed & Breakfast**   (803) 671-5486
P.O. Box 4885
Hilton Head Island, SC 29938

● **Historic Charleston Bed & Breakfast**   (803) 722-6606
43 Legare Street
Charleston, SC 29401

SOUTH DAKOTA

● **Bed & Breakfast of South Dakota**   (605) 528-6571
P.O. Box 80137
Sioux Falls, SD 57116

TENNESSEE

- **Bed & Breakfast in Memphis** (901) 726-5920
P.O. Box 41621
Memphis, TN 38104

- **Bed & Breakfast, Inc.** (615) 522-2337
P.O. Box 2701
Knoxville, TN 37901

- **Grinders Switch B&B Reservation Agency** (615) 729-5002
Rt. 2, P.O. Box 44
Centerville, TN 37033

- **Hospitality at Home, Inc.** (615) 693-3500
Rt. 1, Buttermilk Road
P.O. Box 318
Lenoir City, TN 37771

- **Nashville Bed & Breakfast** (615) 298-5674
P.O. Box 150651
Nashville, TN 37215

- **Nashville Host Homes (a B&B Group)** (615) 331-5244
P.O. Box 110227
Nashville, TN 37222-0227

- **River Rendezvous** (901) 767-5296
P.O. Box 240001
Memphis, TN 38124
Citywide.

TEXAS

- **Bed & Breakfast Hosts of San Antonio** (512) 824-8036
166 Rockhill
San Antonio, TX 78209

- **Bed & Breakfast Society of Houston** (713) 666-6372
4432 Holt Street
Bellaire, TX 77401

- **Bed & Breakfast Texas Style** (214) 298-8586/5433
4224 W. Red Bird Lane
Dallas, TX 75237
B&Bs cover the entire state.

● *Gasthaus Bed & Breakfast Lodgings*   (512) 997-4712
330 W. Main Street
Fredericksburg, TX 78624

● *Sanddollar Hospitality*   (512) 853-1222
3605 Mendenhall
Corpus Christi, TX 78415
B&Bs within the Padre Island area.

UTAH

● *Bed & Breakfast Association of Utah*   (801) 532-7076
P.O. Box 81062
Salt Lake City, UT 84108

VERMONT

● *American Bed & Breakfast*   (802) 524-4731
P.O. Box 983
St. Albans, VT 05478
*Throughout the Northeast, including New Hampshire, Mas-
sachusetts, and New York.*

● *Vermont Bed & Breakfast Referral Service*   (802) 899-2354
P.O. Box 139, Browns Trace
Jericho, VT 05465

VIRGINIA

● *Bed & Breakfast of Tidewater, Virginia*   (804) 627-1983 or 9409
P.O. Box 3343
Norfolk, VI 23514
*Covers Virginia's eastern shore, Norfolk, Portsmouth, Chesapeake,
and Virginia Beach.*

● *Bensonhouse of Richmond*   (804) 648-7560 or 321-6277
P.O. Box 15131
Richmond, VA 23227
B&Bs in other areas of Virginia as well.

● *Blue Ridge Bed & Breakfast*   (703) 955-1246
Rt. 2, P.O. Box 259, Rocks & Rills
Berryville, VA 22611
B&Bs west of Washington, D.C.

● *Guesthouses Reservation Service*　　　　　(804) 979-7264
P.O. Box 5737
Charlottesville, VA 22905
B&B surrounding Charlottesville. Also private guesthouses.

● *Princely Bed & Breakfast Ltd.*　　　　　(703) 683-2159
819 Prince Street
Alexandria, VA 22314
Covers areas from the White House to Alexandria and Mt. Vernon and beyond.

● *Shenandoah Valley Bed & Breakfast*　　　　(703) 896-9702
P.O. Box 305
Broadway, VA 22815
Homes between the Alleghenies and Blue Ridge Mountains.

● *Sojourners Bed & Breakfast*　　　　　(804) 384-1655
3609 Tanglewood Lane
Lynchburg, VA 24503
Lists homes in Central Virginia and the Blue Ridge Mountains.

● *The Travel Tree*　　　　(804) 229-6477 or 565-2236
P.O. Box 838
Williamsburg, VA 23187
Homes in Williamsburg, Yorktown, Jamestown, etc.

WASHINGTON

● *BABS (Bed & Breakfast Service)*　　　　(206) 733-8642
P.O. Box 5025
Bellingham, WA 98227
Nationwide accommodations, modestly priced in the European tradition.

● *Pacific Bed & Breakfast*　　　　(206) 784-0539
701 N.W. Sixtieth Street
Seattle, WA 98107
Covers the Pacific Northwest, including Reno, Puget Sound, and British Columbia.

● *RSVP Bed & Breakfast Reservation Service*　　　　(206) 384-6586
P.O. Box 778
Ferndale, WA 98248
Covers areas from Washington into Canada.

● *Travellers' Bed & Breakfast*   (206) 232-2345
P.O. Box 492
Mercer Island, WA 98040
Homes in Seattle, Vancouver, British Columbia, and Washington.

● *Whidby Island Bed & Breakfast*   (206) 221-8709
P.O. Box 459
Langley, WA 98260

WISCONSIN

● *Bed & Breakfast in Door Country*   (414) 743-9742
Route 2
Algoma, WI 54201

● *Bed & Breakfast of Milwaukee, Inc.*   (414) 342-5030
3017 N. Downer Avenue
Milwaukee, WI 53211

CHAPTER 12

Sources and Resources

Consultants

Perhaps the most ideal advisors, consultants are experts in their fields, usually having practiced what they are preaching. Since consultants are specialists, their fees are often high. Consultants, however, can answer specific questions; one-on-one meetings produce immediate information that is of particular value to the student, especially when pertinent questions are submitted in advance of the appointment. (If possible, this should always be done, for if the expert has to research, it won't be on the client's time. When paying by the hour, dollars fly along with the minutes. At the very least, bring along a carefully thought-out list of points to be covered.)

When looking for a consultant, don't neglect the experience gained by one who is retired or has "failed" in business. I recently sat on the panel of a UCLA business seminar, and found that the most informative speaker was a woman who, just six months earlier, had owned a thriving business. She was fascinating as she described events leading to the dissolution of a dream. We all gained invaluable insight and strength from her reality.

For general and basic business problems, a unique service is offered by the American Woman's Economic Development Corporation (AWED), a non-profit corporation that charges amazingly low fees because it is partially underwritten by the Small Business Administration and by major U.S. companies and foundations. AWED counselors have vast experience in every phase of business growth, development, and management for both product and service businesses, including: finance, accounting, sales, design, personnel, and public relations. Counseling sessions are offered at the New York offices (an hour to an hour and a half: $25.00), by telephone for the same cost (they pay the phone bill), and via a unique "hotline" for women entrepreneurs nationwide. Each hotline session is designed to answer a single question, lasts up to ten minutes, and costs just $5.00. For further information, contact:

American Woman's Economic Development Corporation
The Lincoln Building
60 E. Forty-second Street   (800) 222-AWED
New York, NY 10165   (800) 442-AWED (in NY state)
In New York City, Alaska, and Hawaii, call (212) 692-9100.

For readers in the New York area, AWED offers an 18-month, 9-session course for women who are just starting out, but already know what kind of business they want to get into. The cost: $175. Another course, "How to Manage Your Own Business," is for active business owners (of at least six months) and includes on-site management analysis. Cost: $350. An intermediate program is offered as well.

I suggest a visit to many B&B inns and Homestays. A follow-up call or letter to the host you find most enjoyable, and whose operation you would like to emulate, will doubtless provide an ideal consultant and mentor. Consultations can be held in person, by mail, via long-distance phone, or a combination of all three. Listed here are consultants whom I know are currently providing this service. Others may be equally proficient and available—check industry newsletters.

● *Bed & Breakfast Innkeepers Guild*   (805) 966-0589
P.O. Box 20246   (805) 682-2121
Santa Barbara, CA 93120
Personal consultation with three innkeepers, primarily for potential innkeepers. Specific questions are answered in depth. A packet of materials is included with consultation. $100 per hour, with a two-hour minimum.

163

● *Beverly Mathews*   (818) 761-3386
4326 Bellaire Avenue
Studio City, CA 91604
I give personalized, one-on-one consultation for potential Homestay hosts, and follow-up help for those in business. Some innkeeping advice offered. Mail and long-distance phone consultations available at the same rate. Materials packet included. $35.00 per hour (two-hour minimum).

Apprenticeships and Seminars

See the "Primarily for Innkeepers" chapter for seminars that could be worthwhile for Homestay hosts as well, particularly if the idea of commercial innkeeping is part of your future dreams.

Bed & Breakfast Newsletters

For readers who are seriously considering becoming Homestay hosts as well as those opening an inn, I suggest you read as much as possible. Keeping up with the numerous B&B newsletters can help you avoid costly mistakes, and stay abreast of current B&B events. These newsletters also offer excellent public relations and advertising opportunities at little or no cost.

● *Bed & Breakfast Update Newsletter*   (818) 761-3386
P.O. Box 4814   Beverly Mathews
North Hollywood, CA 91607
Cost: $18.00 year (published bi-monthly).
Six-page newsletter condenses the latest information on B&B from over one hundred sources into a single, easy-to-read publication. News for the Homestay host, Reservation Service Operator, and traveler. Free classified ads for subscribers. Written by this author.

● *California Inns*   (707) 542-INNS
P.O. Box 3383   Toby Smith
Santa Rosa, CA 95402
Cost: $20.00 year (published ten times yearly).
Each issue describes in minute detail a selected California inn, leaving the reader with the feeling of having actually had the experience with Ms. Smith. "News Notes" section gives current happenings on the inn scene.

● **Inn Review**   (815) 939-3509
111 E. Court Street, P.O. Box 1789
Kankakee, IL 60901
Cost: $16 charter subscription (10 issues).
"The newsletter of country inns and small hotels." A newsletter for travelers. Six pages of travel news, book reviews, and inn information. Sample copy: $2.00

● **Innkeeping**   (415) 663-8459
P.O. Box 267   Mary E. Davies
Inverness, CA 94937
Cost: $36.00 year (published monthly)
Crammed with technical information for commercial innkeepers and those considering the purchase of an inn. Includes an interview with an innkeeper each month.

● **Bed & Breakfast World**   (512) 997-4712
300 West Main Street
Fredericksburg, TX 78624
A service publication of the Bed & Breakfast Society, sent quarterly at no cost to members and at $2.00 per copy to non-members. Invites letters, stories, and photos. Interviews, book reviews, international B&B information, B&B real estate section, RSO and Homestay information.

● **Innsider Magazine**   (803) 242-5011
P.O. Box 4136
Greenville, SC 29608
Cost: $6.00 year (four issues)
Dedicated to furthering the inn concept, includes purchasing of properties, relevant advertising, inn recipes, interior design ideas, detailed articles on individual inns. Published by an inn broker.

● **Yellow Brick Road**   (714) 680-2236
2445 Northcreek Lane   Bobbi Zane
Fullerton, CA 92631
Cost: $22 year. Single issue $2.00
A newcomer to the newsletter scene, this upbeat monthly is intended for the B&B traveler and includes a calendar of California events, along with B&Bs in the area.

Bed & Breakfast Guides

Once you get started, try to get listed in guides that are appropriate for your area. Some will charge; others are free. No matter. All should be made aware of your existence. Visibility is necessary and promotion can come from the most surprising sources.

- *Bed & Breakfast American Style* ($7.95)
by Norman Simpson
Berkshire Traveller Press, Stockbridge, MA 01262

- *Bed & Breakfast: California* ($7.95)
A Selective Guide
by Linda Kay Bristow
Chronicle Books, San Francisco, CA 94102

- *Bed & Breakfast Homes Directory* ($7.95)
Homes Away from Home—West Coast
by Diane Knight
Knighttime Publications, Cupertino, CA 95014

- *Bed & Breakfast Guide—USA and Canada* ($9.95)
by Phyllis Featherston and Barbara Ostler
National Bed & Breakfast Association, Norwalk, CT 06852

- *Bed & Breakfast in the Northeast*
by Bernice Chesler
Globe Pequot Press, Chester, CT 06412

- *Bed & Breakfast North America* ($10.95)
by Norma Stephens Buzan
Betsy Ross Publications, Bloomfield Hills, MI 48013

- *Bed & Breakfast Northwest* ($7.95)
by Myrna Oakley
Chronicle Books, San Francisco, CA 94102

- *Bed & Breakfast U.S.A.* ($6.95)
All Fifty States Plus Canada
by Betty Rundback and Nancy Kramer
E.P. Dutton, Inc., New York, NY 10016
As a participating member of the Tourist House Association of America (see back of book for application), your facilities will be described in this publication, which has an annual readership of over 25,000.

- *California Bed & Breakfast Book (The)* ($7.95)
by Kathy Strong
East Woods Press, Charlotte, NC 28203

- *Complete Guide to Bed & Breakfasts, Inns & Guesthouses* ($9.95)
by Pamela Lanier
John Muir Publications, Santa Fe, NM 87504

- *Country Inns of America Series* ($6.95 each)
Covering every section of America
The Knapp Press, Los Angeles, CA 90036

- *Country Inns of the Far West ($4.95)*
by Jacqueline Killeen & Charles Miller
101 Productions, San Francisco, CA 94103

- *The East Coast Bed & Breakfast Guide* ($9.95)
New England and The Mid-Atlantic
by Roberta Gardner
Simon & Schuster, New York, NY 10020

- *The Great American Guest House Book* ($8.95)
by John Thaxton
Burt Franklin & Co., New York, NY 10017

- *The Compleat Traveler Series,* including:
    Country Inns & Historic Hotels of the South
    Country Inns & Historic Hotels of the Middle Atlantic States
    Country New England Inns
    Country Inns & Historic Hotels of California and the West
    Country Inns & Historic Hotels of the Midwest & the Rockies
Burt Franklin & Co., New York, NY 10017

- *Historic Country Inns of California* ($8.95)
by Jim Crain
Chronicle Books, San Francisco, CA 94102

- *A Treasury of Bed & Breakfast* ($12.95)
by The American Bed & Breakfast Association, Washington, DC 20026

- *The West Coast Bed & Breakfast Guide* ($9.95)
California-Oregon-Washington
by Courtia Worth and Terry Berger
Simon & Schuster, New York, NY 10020

- *How to Open a Country Inn* ($8.95)
by Karen Etsell with Elaine Brennan
Berkshire Traveller Press, Stockbridge, MA 01262

- *The Guest House Book Series,* including:
  Middle Atlantic States Guest House Book
  New England Guest House Book
  Southern Guest House Book
by Corinne Madden Ross, East Woods Press Books,
Fast & McMillan Publ., Charlotte, NC 28203

CHAPTER 13

Primarily for Innkeepers

Though potential innkeepers will find functional information throughout each chapter, I feel specific mention must be made of available services that can benefit both current inn owners and those contemplating this career decision.

Before committing to a huge mortgage in unknown territory, you can do a lot of research through books, consultation, seminars, and apprenticeships. Learning from another's experiences can eliminate enormous financial and emotional mistakes. Group seminars will be less costly than individual counsel, and apprenticeships will be cheaper yet. I suggest you take baby steps until you fully realize what innkeeping entails.

While reading books and newsletters, do careful market research of the parts of the country that interest you. Local chambers of commerce offer details on how many hotels/motels there are in the area, how many rooms are available, occupancy percentages and needs, etc. The Small Business Administration can be of help here as well. Speak with local realtors and those specializing in sales and rehabilitation of old properties. Do you want to start from scratch, often discovering tremendous stumbling blocks when working with old buildings? Would you prefer a turnkey operation, one in which someone else has done all of the work, readied it for immediate use, and is therefore entitled to a higher selling price and profit? Are you handy enough to do much of the labor yourself—and up to local codes? Will the zoning commission be amenable if rezoning is necessary? Hundreds of questions must be answered. Get trustworthy advisors; make certain they are experts in the fields.

An apprenticeship with a working inn would seem to be the most logical step to start with for anyone contemplating running an inn. Assistant managers are constantly being sought out as are inn-sitters. The latter are usually expected to be experienced, however. Check the ads in *Innkeeping* and other newsletters (see previous chapter). There, too, you will find occasional listings of working inns that are for sale. Question the reasons for selling.

Inquire at nearby inns for an opportunity to apprentice. Few would turn down the offer of free labor! Some inns run structured "hands-on" programs, charging only for room and board. For more information, contact, among others:

Innkeeping Apprenticeship Programs

- Carl Glassman   (215) 862-2570
Wedgwood Inn
111 West Bridge Street
New Hope, PA 18938

- Margaret and Geoff Lobenstine   (413) 967-7798
Wildwood Inn
Ware, MA 01082

Innkeeping Workshops and Seminars

- *The Bed & Breakfast Innkeepers Guild of Santa Barbara*
P.O. Box 20246   (805) 966-0589
Santa Barbara, CA 93120   Costs from $300.00 including room

- *B&B Seminars*
P.O. Box 295 c/o B&B Productions   (707) 963-0852
St. Helena, CA 94574   Costs from $375.00 plus room

- *Chanticleer Bed & Breakfast Inn* (Innkeepers & Associates, Ashland)
Jim & Nancy Beaver   (503) 482-1919
120 Gresham Street
Ashland, OR 97520   Costs from $225 including room

● *William Oates and Associates*   (802) 254-5931
Box 1162
Brattleboro, VT 05301   Costs from $295 plus room
Held periodically at country inns in Vermont and Pennsylvania.

● *The Captain Freeman Inn*
15 Breakwater Road, RR 2   (617) 896-7481
Brewster, MA 02631

● *Wedgwood Inn of New Hope*
111 West Bridge Street   (215) 862-2570
New Hope, PA 18938

● *Brown's Farm B&B*   (509) 548-7863
Wendi Brown
11150 Highway 209
Leavenworth, WA 98826

For additional workshops and seminars, contact your nearest inn or Innkeepers' Association, and the extension divisions of nearby colleges or universities.

Most innkeeping seminars will include such topics as: finding, financing, and operating an inn; renovation; reservation systems; policies and procedures; employees; security; insurance; government regulations; tours of existing B&B inns; decorating; and may or may not include room and meals.

Some seminars offer more than others at comparable cost. Some provide information you might accumulate from individual specialists at less cost. I suggest collecting brochures with detailed information about content and make a cost-to-value judgment based on subjects covered and speakers' credentials.

B&B and Inn Real Estate Broker/Specialists:

● *The Victorian Register*   (213) 734-1949
Mr. Jim Dunham, owner
1314 W. Twenty-fifth Street
Los Angeles, CA 90007

● *Country Inns Unlimited*   (803) 242-5011
Mr. Jim Casteel
P.O. Box 4136
Greenville, SC 29608

● **William Oates & Associates**   (802) 254-5931
Box 1162
Brattleboro, VT 05301

Countless other specialists in inn real estate exist. Realtors in every city have cooperating brokers throughout the company who will share listings and sales information.

Major cities have preservation groups anxious to retain old structures. These would be the ideal groups to contact about available edifices.

The Preservation News, the monthly newspaper of the National Trust for Historic Preservation, is an excellent source for locating historic properties, as well as for advertising your B&B. Membership: $15.00 per year. Write: National Trust for Historic Preservation, 1785 Massachusetts Avenue, N.W., Washington, DC 20036.

Rehabilitate Old Buildings

Have you ever thought about rehabilitating an old building?

An interesting property could generate publicity. It makes good newspaper material. Rumors abound about the history of many B&Bs. Some were believed to have been used by illegal aliens building the railroads; others were hideaways for rumrunners during Prohibition days, many were lodgings for loggers, traveling salesmen, gold diggers.

● Was the wine cellar of the Hotel Leger, Mokelumne Hill, California really a tunnel to the bordello across the street?

● Was the Cobweb Palace, Westport, California a hippie haven in the sixties?

● Cornell House in Lenox, Massachusetts is said to have been a speakeasy during Prohibition.

● Howard Creek Ranch in Westport, California and The Turning Point, in Great Barrington, Massachusetts were two old stagecoach stops.

● An eighteenth-century gristmill in Pennsylvania is now a B&B.

● The Olde Post Inn was both a post office and customs house in Cold Springs, New York.

- The lighthouse in San Francisco Bay, East Brother, in Point Richmond, California is one of the most exclusive B&Bs in the country.

- The Old Dennis House in Newport, Rhode Island is still a church rectory.

- I wrote earlier of the wonders of Sunnyside, in Sunnyvale, California, a one-time potato chip factory.

The list goes on, but the point is that historic and nonhistoric properties built prior to 1944 and in need of renovation are excellent tax incentives for business ventures. The publicity value is obvious.

Extra-Income Ideas from Practicing Innkeepers

- The Shoreham Inn and Country Store in Shoreham, Vermont, has a small deli and country store.

- Maple Crest Farm in Shrewsbury, Vermont is a working diary farm.

- Catering services and cooking schools are operated out of several B&Bs, making further use of their commercial kitchens.

- Artists in-residence work at the Bangert's Farmhouse in Santa Cruz, California, where visitors can look over their wares.

- American crafts are sold at The Olde Post Inn, Cold Springs, New York.

- The owners of Gallery Osgood in Napa, California display and sell their work and the work of others in the main rooms of their B&B.

- New Davenport Bed & Breakfast, Davenport, California, has a pottery and craft gallery, and serves breakfast and lunch next door at their Cash Store.

- The Carter House's main floor serves as an antique and art gallery. Everything throughout the house is for sale at this Eureka, California inn.

- Weddings and wedding photographs are a constant activity at The Rose Victorian, Arroyo Grande, California, where magnificent rose gardens create additional income.

• Lizzie's handmade apricot soaps and lotions are available for purchase at this Port Townsend, Washington inn.

Innkeeper Resources

• *Innkeeping World*   Charles Nolte
P.O. Box 84108
Seattle, WA 98124
Cost: $37.00 (ten issues) yearly.
An international publication for hotel executives. Covers trends, travel news, ideas culled from major hotels, and descriptions of lodging "classics" in each issue.

• *Guest Services—500 Ideas*   ($10.00)
by the same publisher. Creative ideas from the "Big guys" in the hotel industry. Unique services and amenities, adaptable to inns.

• *American Hotel and Motel Association*
888 Seventh Avenue   (212) 265-4506
New York, NY 10010
A membership organization with a monthly magazine (available to non-members also) for the lodging industry. Offers management courses through the Educational Institute at 1407 S. Harrison Road, East Lansing, MI 48823. Also sponsors annual one-week hotel management seminars on Michigan State University campus, East Lansing.

• *New York University's School of Continuing Education*
50 W. Fourth Street, New York, NY 10003
Offers intensive courses in hotel and motel management.

• **The Bed & Breakfast Innkeepers of Northern California** have a well-attended annual conference, bringing innkeepers and hopefuls from around the country. Held in January of each year, the conferences include such workshops as Promotion; Personnel; Innkeeping 101: From the Beginning; Goal Management; and Marketing as part of the two-day agenda. Speakers are impressive; exhibitors, numerous; fees, reasonable. Contact the Association of Bed & Breakfast Innkeepers of San Francisco, 737 Buena Vista West, San Francisco, CA 94117 for information on next year's "Inn Business" conference.

● *How to Make Money at Innkeeping*   ($29.95)
by Michael Vincent Kuntz
Southern Hospitality Concept, Inc.   (212) 658-0613
142-02 Eighty-fourth Drive
Briarwood, NY 11435
Details budgeting, housekeeping, front desk and reservations, security, food and restaurant departments, etc. for medium to large-sized operations. Author's background in hotel management and consulting is extensive.

● *Cornell University's School of Hotel Administration*
Ithaca, NY 14850
Offers a summer program in hotel/restaurant management with a large choice of short courses (one to three weeks) at $450 weekly, including lodging.

● *Florida International University*
School of Hotel, Food, and Travel Services
Miami, FL 33144

Florida State University
Department of Hotel and Restaurant Management
Tallahassee, FL 32306

● *Michigan State University*
School of Hotel, Restaurant, and Institutional Management
East Lansing, Michigan 48823

Correspondence Courses in management, professional cooking, food service and purchasing, etc., can be taken through accredited schools including Purdue University Continuing Education Business Office, Room 110, Stewart Center, West Lafayette, IN 47907.

CHAPTER 14

For Canadian Readers

Reservation Services

● *Alberta Bed & Breakfast*   (403) 462-8885
4327 Eighty-Sixth Street
Edmonton, Alberta, T6K 1A9
B&B throughout Calgary and Edmonton, Banff, Lake Louise, etc.

● *All Season Bed & Breakfast Agency*   (604) 595-BEDS-5952337
2440 Foul Bay Road   592-8170
Victoria, B.C. V8R 5A9
Specializing in waterfront and garden homes.

● *Bed & Breakfast Kingston Area*   (613) 542-0214
10 Westview Road
Kingston, Ontario K7M 2C3
Ontario, Bath, Westport, Perth, Kingston, and other areas.

● *Born Free Bed & Breakfast Agency*   (604) 298-8815
4390 Frances Street
Burnaby, B.C. V5C 2R3
Homes available throughout British Columbia.

● *Information Orrillia*   (705) 487-3135
71 Mississaga Street W.   (705) 326-7743
Orillia, Ontario L3V 3A8

● *Metropolitan Bed & Breakfast Registry of Toronto*   (416) 964-2566
309 St. George Street   (416) 928-2833
Toronto, Ontario M5R 2R2
Lists host homes in directory; traveler books direct.

● *Montreal Bed & Breakfast*   (514) 738-9410
5020 St. Kevin Suite 8   (514) 738-3859
Montreal, Quebec H3W 1P4

● *Montrealers at Home*   (514) 932-9690
3458 Rue Laval
Montreal, Quebec H2X 3C8
Specializes in downtown Montreal and landmarks in Quebec City.

● *Niagara Region Bed & Breakfast Service*   (416) 358-8988
2631 Dorchester Road
Niagara Falls, Ontario L2J 2Y9

● *The Old English Bed & Breakfast Registry*   (604) 986-5069
363 E. Eighth Street   (604) 943-8241
North Vancouver, B.C. V7L 1Z2
B&Bs throughout Vancouver and British Columbia.

● *Ottawa Area Bed & Breakfast*   (613) 563-0161
P.O. Box 4848 Station "E"
Ottawa, Ontario K1S 5J1
City, suburban, and country homes in Canada's capital.

● *Toronto Bed & Breakfast*   (416) 920-2214
P.O. Box 74, Station "M"
Toronto, Ontario M6S 4T2
*Sells host directory; guests book direct (guests from outside North
America may have selections made by Toronto B&B).*

● *Town & Country Bed & Breakfast in B.C.*   (604) 731-5942
P.O. Box 46544, Station "G"
Vancouver, B.C. V6R 4G6
Offers placement service and sells directory of homes.

● *VIP Bed & Breakfast*   (604) 477-5604
1786 Teakwood Road
Victoria, B.C. V8N 1E2
Homes near city center, university, waterfront, and airport.

● *Victoria Hospitality Club*   (604) 381-2312
Building One—841 Fairfield Road
Victoria, B.C. V8V 3B6
*A seniors' volunteer project to facilitate holiday travel accommoda-
tions for seniors and visitors of all ages.*

● *Victoria Bed & Breakfast, Inc.*　　　　　(604) 385-2332
209–703 Broughton Street
Victoria, B.C. V8W 1E2
Locations throughout Victoria.

The Canadian Government and Ministry of Tourism and Recreation recognize the importance of B&B. Each province provides considerable material for the asking. Contact the bureaus in your home area for information on how to be included in such literature. In addition, many books, published both in Canada and the United States, should be considered for publicity and advertising purposes. Canada also has numerous membership associations for potential hosts. A representative group of RSOs is listed above, and there are several others throughout the country. Start investigating.

Books and Brochures Available for Canadian B&B

B&B brochures are available from the following sources:

● *Nova Scotia Department of Tourism*
Box 130
Halifax, Nova Scotia B3J 2MJ
Bed & Breakfast is sponsored by the government and includes fifty-six island homes. Rates are fixed on these Cape Breton B&Bs.

● *Accommodation Guide to British Columbia*
Tourism British Columbia
3400 Wilshire Boulevard No. 34 Arcade
Los Angeles, CA 90010

● *Bed & Breakfast Accommodation in Stratford and Area*
A Stratford and Area Visitors' and Convention Bureau publication.
　Write to:
Stratford and Area Visitors' and Convention Bureau
38 Albert Street　　　　　　　　　　　　(519) 271-5140
Stratford, Ontario N5A 3K3

- Ontario/Canada Bed & Breakfast Associations will also provide brochures printed, but not licensed by, the Ministry of Tourism. Write:

Ontario Travel
Queen's Park, Toronto, Ontario M7A 2R9

- *The Canadian Bed & Breakfast Guide*
  $10.95 plus $1.00 handling (Canadian)
  by Gerda Pantel Fitzhenry and Whiteside Publishers
  195 Allstate Parkway   (416) 477-0030
  Markham, Ontario L3R 4T8

- *A Travellers Guide to Canadian Bed & Breakfast Places*
  by John Thompson & Patricia Wilson $12.95 (Canadian)
  Grosvenor House Press   (416) 364-5510
  75 Sherbourne Street
  Toronto, Ontario M5A 2P9

- *Bed & Breakfast in Ontario* $8.95 (U.S. or Canadian)
  by Patricia Wilson
  Clarke Irwin, Inc.
  Box 200
  Agincourt, Ontario M1S 3B6

- *Country Bed & Breakfast Places in Canada*
  compiled by John Thompson $9.95
  Berkshire Traveller Press   (413) 298-3636
  Stockbridge, MA 01262

- *Town & Country Bed & Breakfast in B.C.*
  by Helen Birch & Pauline Scoten $5.95
  T&C Publishers
  P.O. Box 46544 Station "G"
  Vancouver, B.C. 4G6

- *Lodges & Historic Hotels of Canada* $6.95
  by Anthony Hitchcock and Jean Lindgren   (212) 687-5250
  Publisher: Burt Franklin & Co.
  235 E. Forty-fourth Street
  New York, NY 10017

● *Sleep Cheap* $6.95
compiled by Jon and Nancy Kugelman
c/o McBride/Publisher
157 Sisson Avenue
Hartford, CT 06105

Additional Visitor and Tourism Services to Contact

● *Travel Arctic*
Yellowknife, NW X1A 229 Canada

● *Tourism British Columbia*
1117 Wharf Street, Victoria, B.C. V8W 272

● *Kensington Area Tourist Association*   (902) 836-5418
Prince Edward Island, RR1, Kensington, PEI COB 1MO Can

● *New Brunswick Tourism*
P.O. Box 12345, Frederick, New Brunswick E3B 5C3, Canada

● *Visitors Services Division*
P.O. Box 940, Charlottetown, PE C1A 7MJ Canada

● *Tourist Services Division*
Box 2061, St. John's, Newfoundland A1C 5R8 Canada

● *Tourism Yukon*
Box 2703, Whitehouse, Yukon Y1A 2C6

● *Minister of Industry & Commerce*
Tourism Dept. 150 E. Cyrille Blvd., Quebec G1R 4Y3

● *Office of Tourism*
5629 Fall Avenue, Niagara Falls, Ontario, L2E 3P7 Canada

Afterword

On the one hand, I know *Start Your Own Bed & Breakfast Business* will open up a world of ideas for adventuresome readers. On the other, I fear I may have gone into such detail that some of you will finish this book thinking that B&B hosting is far too complicated for you. I am simply trying to cover all bases and provide answers for questions that might never come up for you. Don't be afraid to try B&B if the idea appeals to you at all. You can always change your mind. There is little to lose.

One of my RSO owners and her husband are being followed by a TV documentary crew as I sit here writing. The couple is over fifty and starting their *third* career. Through their letters and their travels they exude the joy of adventure and youth. As a local radio psychologist admonishes, life is not a dress rehearsal. We are living right now, today, and this is the only "now" we will ever have. We cannot turn around and reshoot the scene that has played. This is it!

I plan to continue finding the newness and excitement in each "today" I have, and hope that you will too. B&Bing is just one way to start.

Help!

Dear Beverly:
After reading your book, I have a few specific questions that need some answers when you have the time.

NAME: _____

ADDRESS: _____

Complete and return together with a self-addressed, stamped envelope to:
Beverly Mathews
P.O. Box 4814
North Hollywood, CA 91607-4814
Actual page must accompany requests for information; no Xerox copies will be answered. This service is offered solely to the buyer of this book.
Please cut carefully on dotted line and return. Leave room on page for my reply.

_____

_____

_____

_____

_____

_____

_____

_____

_____

_____

Reservation Service Updated Information Request

Dear Beverly:
I have contacted all of the national reservation services and those listed under my state. Is there any new information of which I should be aware? If so, please let me know.

NAME ⎯⎯⎯⎯⎯⎯⎯⎯⎯⎯⎯⎯⎯⎯⎯⎯⎯⎯⎯⎯⎯

ADDRESS ⎯⎯⎯⎯⎯⎯⎯⎯⎯⎯⎯⎯⎯⎯⎯⎯⎯⎯⎯⎯

STATE ⎯⎯⎯⎯⎯⎯⎯⎯⎯⎯⎯⎯⎯⎯⎯⎯⎯⎯⎯⎯⎯

STATES (IF ANY) MY TOWN/CITY BORDERS ON: ⎯⎯⎯⎯

Complete and return together with a self-addressed stamped envelope to:
Beverly Mathews
P.O. Box 4814
North Hollywood, CA 91607-4814
Leave room below for Beverly's reply. (Please cut carefully on dotted line to preserve your book.)

Special Subscription Offer
Bed & Breakfast Update Newsletter

For those who have purchased this book, I am offering a special *extended* subscription to *Bed & Breakfast Update*, the bi-monthly newsletter that condenses the latest information on B&B from over one hundred sources into one easy-to-read publication. Save time and money. Get the best of the latest news. For the Homestay host, traveler, reservation service organizations, innkeepers! Regular subscription price $18.00/6 issues.

Detach and return this page (no Xerox copies please) for two extra *free* issues.

Cut carefully

Please start my subscription to *Bed & Breakfast Update* with the current issue. I understand that I am eligible for *eight* issues instead of the usual six.

NAME _____

ADDRESS _____

CITY _____

STATE _____ZIP _____ PHONE _____

Please make check or money order in the amount of $18.00 U.S. dollars, payable to: *Bed & Breakfast Update*. Return to: *Bed & Breakfast Update*, P.O. Box 4814, North Hollywood, CA 91607. This purchase may be tax-deductible when used in connection with your business or profession. Outside U.S./Canada, please add $5.00 (U.S.) for postage/handling.

In the section on networking (see Chapter 8), I mention the importance of professional contacts in making a B&B a success. You may want to apply to the Tourist House Association of America for membership.

THE TOURIST HOUSE ASSOCIATION OF AMERICA APPLICATION FOR MEMBERSHIP

(Please type or print)

Name of Bed & Breakfast: _____

Address: _____

City: _____State: _____Zip: _____Phone: ( ) _____

Best Time to Call: _____

Host(s): _____

Located: No. of miles _____ Compass Direction _____ of

Major City _____

No. of miles _____from Major Route _____

Accommodations: Total number of guest bedrooms: _____

Total number of private baths:_____

Maximum number of guests who must share one bathroom: _____

Room Rates:

$____Double—private bath $____Double—shared bath
$____Single—private bath $____Single—shared bath
$____Children 12 or under $____Suites
Separate Guest Cottage $____Sleeps ____

Are you open year-round?   ☐ Yes   ☐ No
If "No," specify when you are open: _____

Do you discount rates at any time?   ☐ No   ☐ Yes   If "Yes," specify (i.e., 10% less during March, April, November; 15% less than daily rate if guests stay a week; $10 less per night Sunday through Thursday)._____
Do you offer a discount to senior citizens?   ☐ No   ☐ Yes: ____ %
Do you offer a discount for families?   ☐ No   ☐ Yes: ____ %

Breakfast: Type of breakfast included in rate:
☐ Full   ☐ Continental
Breakfast is not included: ☐ cost: $ ____

Are any other meals provided?　☐ No　☐ Yes
Lunch ☐ cost: $——————— Dinner ☐ cost: $———————

Meals are included in rate quoted with room　☐ Yes　☐ No

Do you accept Credit Cards?　☐ No　☐ Yes:
☐ AMEX　☐ DINERS　☐ MASTERCARD　☐ VISA

Will you GUARANTEE your rates from January through December, 1986? ( ) Yes ( ) No

Note: This Guarantee applies only to those guests making reservations having read about you in *Bed & Breakfast USA.*

Do you have household pets? ☐ Dog　☐ Cat　☐ Bird
Can you accommodate a guest's pet?
☐ Yes　☐ No　☐ Sometimes
Are children welcome?　☐ No　☐ Yes If "Yes," any age restriction?————————————————————————————

Do you permit smoking in your house?　☐ Yes　☐ No
Do you object to social drinking?　☐ Yes　☐No

Guests can be met at　☐ Airport ——　☐ Train ——　☐ Bus——

Can you speak a foreign language fluently?　☐ No ☐ Yes

Describe: ————————————————————————

GENERAL AREA OF YOUR B&B (i.e., Boston Historic District; 20 minutes from Chicago Loop):

GENERAL DESCRIPTION OF YOUR B&B (i.e., brick colonial with white shutters; Victorian mansion with stained-glass windows):

AMBIENCE OF YOUR B&B (i.e., furnished with rare antiques; lots of wood and glass):

THE QUALITIES THAT MAKE YOUR B&B SPECIAL ARE:

THINGS OF HISTORIC, SCENIC, CULTURAL, OR GENERAL INTEREST NEARBY (i.e., 1 mile from the San Diego Zoo; walking distance to the Lincoln Memorial):

YOUR OCCUPATION and SPECIAL INTERESTS (i.e., a retired teacher of Latin interested in woodworking; full-time hostess interested in quilting):

If you do welcome children, are there any special provisions for them (i.e., crib, playpen, highchair, play area, baby-sitter)?

Breakfast is prepared by ☐ Host ☐ Guest
Breakfast specialties of the house are (i.e., homemade breads and jams; blueberry pancakes):

Do you offer snacks (i.e., complimentary wine and cheese; pretzels and chips but BYOB)?

Can guests use your kitchen for light snacks? ☐ Yes ☐ No
Do you offer the following amenities: ☐ Guest Refrigerator
☐ Air-conditioning ☐ TV ☐ Piano ☐ Washing Machine
☐ Dryer ☐ Sauna ☐ Pool ☐ Tennis Court Other_____

What major college or university is within 10 miles?
_____

Do you offer a discount for other B&B hosts in our Association?
☐ No ☐ Yes: ____%

Please supply the name, address, and phone number of three personal references from people not related to you (please use a separate sheet).

Please enclose a copy of your brochure, if possible, along with a photo of your B&B. If you have a black and white line drawing, send it along too. If you have a special breakfast recipe that you'd like to share, send it along too. (Of course, credit will be given to your B&B.) Nobody can describe your B&B better than you. If you'd like to try your hand, please do so. We will of course reserve the right to edit. As a member of the Tourist House Association of America, your B&B will be described in the next edition of our book, *BED & BREAKFAST USA*, published by E. P. Dutton, Inc. and distributed to bookstores and libraries throughout the U.S. The book is also used as a reference for B&Bs in our country by major offices of tourism throughout the world.

Note: If the publisher or authors receive negative reports from your guests regarding a deficiency in our standards of CLEANLINESS, COMFORT, and CORDIALITY, we reserve the right to cancel your Membership.

This Membership Application has been prepared by:

_____
(Signature)

Please enclose your $15 Membership Dues.   Date:_____

Return to:
Tourist House Association of America
Box 355A, R.D. 2
Greentown, PA 18426

- -

THE TOURIST HOUSE
ASSOCIATION OF AMERICA
APPLICATION FOR MEMBERSHIP FOR A
BED & BREAKFAST RESERVATION SERVICE

NAME OF BED & BREAKFAST SERVICE: _____
ADDRESS: _____
CITY: _____STATE: _____ZIP: _____PHONE: (   ) _____
BEST TIME TO CALL: _____
COORDINATOR: _____

Names of State(s), Cities, and Towns where you have Hosts (in alphabetical order, please, and limit to 10):

Number of Hosts on your roster: _____

THINGS OF HISTORIC, SCENIC, CULTURAL, OR GENERAL INTEREST IN THE AREA(S) YOU SERVE:

Range of Rates:

Modest:	Single $_____	Double $_____
Average:	Single $_____	Double $_____
Luxury:	Single $_____	Double $_____

Will you GUARANTEE your rates through December, 1986?
( ) Yes   ( ) No

Do you accept Credit Cards?   ☐ No   ☐ Yes:
☐ AMEX   ☐ DINERS   ☐ MASTERCARD   ☐ VISA

Is the guest required to pay a fee to use your service?
☐ No   ☐ Yes—The fee is $_____

Do you publish a Directory of your B&B listings?
☐ No   ☐ Yes—The fee is $_____

Are any of your B&Bs within 10 miles of a university? Which?__

Briefly describe a sample Host Home in each of the above categories: e.g., a cozy farmhouse where the host weaves rugs; a restored 1800 Victorian where the host is a retired general; a contemporary mansion with a sauna and swimming pool.

Please supply the name, address, and phone number of three personal references from people not related to you (please use a separate sheet of paper). Please enclose a copy of your brochure. This Membership Application has been prepared by:

_____
(Signature)

Please enclose your $15 Membership Dues.   Date:_____

If you have a special breakfast recipe that you'd like to share, send it along. (Of course, credit will be given to your B&B agency.) As a member of the Tourist House Association of America, your B&B agency will be described in the next edition of our book, *BED & BREAKFAST USA*, published by E. P. Dutton, Inc.

Return to:
Tourist House Association
R.D. 2, Box 355A
Greentown, PA 18426